"There is a dizzying litany of [...] rary marketplace. Many of th[...] so much. But far too few have been penned to help us know *how* we relate to God. In the rugged history of Christianity, some of our heroes and saints have offered beautiful descriptions of how they found the God of Scripture. Their tales are so needed today. This book mines our history and theology for these tested and true gifts. I commend Sherrill's miraculous book. And I believe God will show you a whole new way to know him."

—**A. J. Swoboda**, assistant professor, Bushnell University; author of *After Doubt*

"I first met AJ Sherrill somewhere on the streets of a noisy, busy city. Now, some years later, I find myself rejoicing in AJ as an emerging voice on how to quiet the noise and find rest in the busy places. If you are looking for a field guide to help you enter into the rest of Christ, look no further. This is that field guide."

—**Scott Sauls**, senior pastor, Christ Presbyterian Church; author of *Jesus Outside the Lines* and *A Gentle Answer*

"In a world filled with distractions, Christians are often people of action but not too often people of contemplation and prayer. This approach ultimately results in stress, depression, and burnout. More than ever, we need to rediscover contemplative prayer that will help sustain us for living in today's complex and changing world. *Being with God* is a timely book filled with timeless wisdom for today's church. Read it, contemplate it, but most of all, practice it!"

—**Winfield Bevins**, director of church planting, Asbury Seminary; author of *Ever Ancient, Ever New*

"This is a fantastic book for those pursuing the way of Jesus. Instead of adding another religious task to do, AJ seeks to instill the necessity of being with God. Truly abiding is a forgotten discipline in our time from which all spiritual fruit is born. I highly recommend this book."

—**Jon Tyson**, lead pastor, Trinity Grace Church

"Sherrill pastorally calls for Christians to disentangle themselves from the loud clamoring of the world by embracing the formational rhythms of Jesus and entering into the depths of a gracious, loving, and kind God. AJ not only casts the vision, he also pastorally tells us how to experience the fullness of God."

—**Tara Beth Leach**, author of *Emboldened* and *Radiant Church*

"I'm addicted. Addicted to activity. Addicted to noise. Addicted to accomplishment. All this addiction means I'm never still. My mind never quiets. I often lack the space to be with God. And, crazy as it sounds, that's what God wants most. AJ gifts the church with needed, helpful insights into the crazed culture we live in and the way our minds work, and he presses it against God's dream for human flourishing. If you, like me, struggle to get quiet, read this book."

—**Sean Palmer**, teaching pastor, Ecclesia Houston; author of *Forty Days on Being a Three* (Enneagram Daily Reflections)

"Feeling like a robot programmed by demanding outside forces? Tired of constant reactivity, of having little capacity to respond functionally to life? Read *Being with God*. Sherrill's insights will reshape your soul, which will in turn reshape your life in the world."

—**Bishop Todd Hunter**, author of *Deep Peace: Finding Calm in a World of Conflict and Anxiety*

BEING WITH GOD

Also by the author

The Enneagram for Spiritual Formation:
How Knowing Ourselves Can Make Us More Like Jesus

BEING

WITH

GOD

THE ABSURDITY, NECESSITY, AND
NEUROLOGY OF CONTEMPLATIVE PRAYER

AJ SHERRILL

BrazosPress

a division of Baker Publishing Group
Grand Rapids, Michigan

Published by Brazos Press
a division of Baker Publishing Group
PO Box 6287, Grand Rapids, MI 49516-6287
www.brazospress.com

Printed in the United States of America

Library of Congress Cataloging-in-Publication Data
Names: Sherrill, Andrew (Andrew Jeremy), author.
Title: Being with God : the absurdity, necessity, and neurology of contemplative prayer / A. J. Sherrill.
Description: Grand Rapids, Michigan : Brazos Press, a division of Baker Publishing Group, [2021] | Includes bibliographical references.
Identifiers: LCCN 2021011627 | ISBN 9781587434730 (paperback) | ISBN 9781587435416 (casebound) | ISBN 9781493432790 (ebook)
Subjects: LCSH: Contemplation. | Prayer—Christianity. | Solitude—Religious aspects—Christianity. | Spirituality—Christianity.
Classification: LCC BV5091.C7 S49 2021 | DDC 248.3/2—dc23
LC record available at https://lccn.loc.gov/2021011627

Author is represented by The Christopher Ferebee Agency, www.christopherferebee.com.

Baker Publishing Group publications use paper produced from sustainable forestry practices and post-consumer waste whenever possible.

21 22 23 24 25 26 27   7 6 5 4 3 2 1

To the Holy Spirit.
You counsel, comfort, and keep us
every moment in this sacred life.
You are the conversation within our being.
May this humble book serve as a living testimony
to your faithful presence in the world.

CONTENTS

PART 3
NEUROLOGY 109

FOREWORD

THOMAS AQUINAS, one of the most important theologians in the history of the church, had a phrase in his classic thirteenth-century work, *Summa Theologiae*, that summed up much of his witness to God: "*Contemplare et contemplata aliis tradere,*" which means, "Contemplate and share the fruit of your contemplation." Eight centuries later, we are in desperate need to revisit this profoundly simple invitation. Why? Because what the world—and many parts of the church—has offered is diametrically opposed to this vision.

Instead of offering fruit from a place of sustained, prayerful abiding in Christ, we are being offered, and thereby offering, the fruit of reactivity, anxiety, and simplistic solutions for a vastly complicated world. What the world—and, more importantly, the church—desperately needs are people who have been with God. People who can offer a quality of presence that disrupts the violent pace that has swallowed many people whole—a presence shaped by contemplation.

The world is in distress in large part because of the quality of our prayers, and consequently the quality of our lives. This is why I'm convinced that if we change how we pray, we can open ourselves to something—or rather someone—who can do something in us that we can't produce in ourselves.

It's for this reason that I'm thrilled about the book you're holding. Every generation needs new words to help us understand what it means to abide deeply in God. We need fresh words from people who have been with God. One of my favorite verses in the New Testament is found in Acts 4. Peter and John are taken captive by the religious guard because of their gospel message. They are put in jail and questioned. In response, Peter goes on to boldly proclaim the redemptive story of Jesus.

After hearing Peter speak, there's an important observation from the religious establishment: "When they saw the courage of Peter and John . . . , they took note that *these men had been with Jesus*" (Acts 4:13). Hear those words: "These men had been with Jesus." What would it look like if the world looked at women and men in this generation and concluded, "These people have been with Jesus"? In our day, it's easier to say, "These people have been with cable news personalities" or "These people have been with some judgmental religious types." But imagine if people could look at our lives—our courageous, loving, nonanxious lives—and only say, "These people have been with Jesus."

In this book, you have a wonderful guide to help you do just that—be with Jesus. And thankfully it's coming from someone who has been with Jesus. AJ Sherrill is not only one of this generation's much-needed voices, he's also a dear friend I've come to deeply admire and respect. I've spent evenings in his home, have had many meals with him, and have had the privilege of partnering with him in various teaching settings. Every time I'm with him, I think, *this guy has been with Jesus.*

AJ has taken seriously the call to abide deeply in Christ and to offer the fruit of that shared presence. He writes with an accessible astuteness, offering wisdom from a deep place of contemplation and nuanced cultural analysis. He presents a beautiful vision of Christian faith that draws me more into the life of

God—which for me is the best compliment I can offer another writer.

In this book, AJ has curated and joined various disciplines and practices to help us draw near to God through contemplative prayer. He's offering a perspective on a topic that too often comes across as ethereal and unattainable. In this book, you'll discover that contemplative prayer is for everyone, no matter where you are in your spiritual journey. I've read many books on contemplative prayer over the years, but I've had a hard time recommending books because most don't meet people where they are. With this book I don't have that problem.

So sit down, take a deep breath, and open yourself to God's presence through these pages. I'm so glad I did.

Rich Villodas

Lead pastor of New Life Fellowship
and author of *The Deeply Formed Life*

INTRODUCTION

Read Me

Talking *at* God
Speaking *to* God
Listening *for* God
Being *with* God

At, to, for, with. These are the four basic ways we pray. Many Christians in the West know the first two (*at* and *to*) rather well, the third (*for*) a fair bit, but the fourth (*with*) hardly at all. It is this fourth mode that I aim to address in this book. Perhaps the great omission of being *with* God in prayer is what prevents the church from growing into the depths of God's heart for the world. Within a culture of external and internal noise, we must learn the rhythms and intimacy of contemplative prayer if we are to flourish.

When asked to describe their prayer life, many people point only to the words they speak to God and the impressions they claim to feel from God. While these are a part of prayer, they only begin to scratch the surface of being with God. The truth is that every moment of every day, the most significant reality in the entire universe is the radical availability of God's presence.

Types of Prayer

Within a spiritual climate that often omits being *with* God, it is inadequate to talk about the problem without offering practical steps to solve it. I have met many who long for a quieter life with God, a stiller soul of peace, and freedom from the pervasive inner chatter but who feel that these longings remain elusive and impractical. When I teach on stillness and rest in the church, particularly in urban contexts, people lean in and nod their heads in agreement. We are tired, longing for respite.

The four types of prayer mentioned above come from Mark Thibodeaux's *Armchair Mystic*, which describes these types of prayer using prepositions:

talking *at* God
speaking *to* God
listening *for* God
being *with* God[1]

When we are young, we are first taught to pray *at* God. As a child, perhaps you kneeled at your bedside to pray, "Now I lay me down to sleep . . ." Or maybe before dinner you launched into a rehearsed prayer from Sunday school that went, "God is great, God is good, thank you, Jesus, for this food." In this mode of prayer, we launch simple phrases toward the sky in hopes of divine reception. God is like a static entity—a God who exists to receive whatever we speak toward heaven.

The next stage of prayer maturity encourages us to pray *to* God. At this stage, we move from viewing God as a static entity to viewing him as a dynamic being. Prayer here becomes a cosmic conversation. Through it, we learn to enter into a dialogue with the divine. For example, in the car or on public transit, we may carry our needs, worries, and fears to God in hopes of experiencing provision, peace, and courage. This stage of prayer begins to feel like more of a spiritual connection. We seek a conversation with a dynamic God who responds to our prayers and can be influenced to act on our behalf and for the sake of others.

As we grow as Christians, we learn to listen *for* God. At this stage, we begin to attune our ears, seek God through Scripture and others, and observe bodily promptings to discern God's voice in a noisy world. Perhaps at this stage we ask, "God, what is your will?" and "What would you like me to do?" Through this form of prayer, we are compelled to hear the Holy Spirit nudge us in specific directions as we navigate life's complexities. For many Christians, prophetic words and divine insight become a part of the faith journey at this point. In the listening-to-God phase of prayer, one comes to discover that the relationship is one of both give and take. It is no different in human relationships, which flourish only when people both speak and listen in turn. Thibodeaux asserts, "This [form of prayer] is often felt by receiving an impression from God, an image that leads us further into something, and/or a word that clarifies what we have been needing to hear or know."[2]

I am not suggesting this is an inevitable, linear path, but it is a typical—and wonderful—path of prayer growth. Each of these stages is good.

But . . . it is here that many Christ followers stop progressing in their prayer pilgrimage. Prayer must become more for us than thinking thoughts about and saying words to God. At some point, our relationship with God demands that we move away from words, away from noise, and away from the mental chatter and toward discovering God in the quiet.

All three of these types of prayer are cataphatic in nature. "Cataphatic" is a fancy word that simply means that it engages one of our five senses in some way. Although the third direction moves us into listening, it is still dependent on images, feelings, and words. To reiterate, these directions are good but incomplete. They are comfortable but lacking. Activist Carlo Carretto wisely said, "This is crucial: as long as we pray only when and how we want to, our life of prayer is bound to be unreal."[3]

There is a fourth stage of prayer that few seek but all of us need. We must learn to be *with* God. At this stage, words are welcomed but not required. Learning the art of being with God, we realize it is enough to be still, to be silent, to be in solitude with the God who knows our hearts, our needs, and our longings. This stage, Thibodeaux contends,

> is radically different from all the others for two reasons. First, it is not an action like talking or listening, but rather is a state of being. It is not so much what I do during my prayer times, but who I've become because of them. Second, because this is not an action that I can do, it is virtually out of my control. Unlike the other stages, I cannot make this stage happen. It must come as a pure gift from God. All I can do is till the soil so that the land will be fertile when the Sower comes to plant the seeds.[4]

This is the all-important stage of surrendering a particular outcome of prayer. No longer do we need to demand that God "show up" for us in a certain way by providing us with a feeling, impression, or word of clarity. It is enough to be with God in this form of prayer. Like Mary, in this type of prayer, we treasure God in our hearts, knowing that is enough.

The Contemplative Journey

This book aims to address and help you experience this fourth way of prayer: being *with* God, practicing stillness, silence, and being as a mode of prayer. Some have called this the practice of contemplation, contemplative prayer, or the contemplative journey. Contemplation is one of the ways Christians experience God's presence. Many Protestants are unfamiliar with this practice, and sometimes understandably so, as contemplation is often conflated with Eastern religious traditions, which omit the necessity of receiving the Spirit of God through the work of Christ's life, death, resurrection, and ascension. Because the word "contemplation" takes on different meanings for various people across religious traditions, I want to be clear from the onset how I use the term throughout this book. Robert Mulholland defines contemplation as simply "the practice of stilling ourselves before God, moving ever deeper into the core of our being and simply offering ourselves to God in totally vulnerable love."[5] I like that definition. This book is about how we begin to do that, specifically with a commitment to the historic Christian faith.

In an age of absurdity in which noise, anxiety, chaos, hurry, and worry dominate the landscape of life, we need to reclaim this kind of praying life and discover via the fantastic world of our neurology how prayer can be the path to holistic healing. Above all, prayer leads us directly into the meaning of the universe—namely, the relational presence of God.

Contemplation may be the most challenging of all the spiritual disciplines of Christian discipleship. Therefore, at the conclusion of each chapter of this book is a practice. The practices suggested are not filler material. Spiritual practices matter, and the greater the repetition, the greater the formation. Conversely stated, where there is little repetition, you can expect little formation.

The aim of this book is to help you gain understanding. But the understanding you will gain is not an end but a means. Spiritual growth is not the measure of one's conceptual knowledge about God but the cultivation of biblical virtue. This cultivation is not like an efficient machine but more like farming. It is a slow but steady growing into Christlikeness over the course of a lifetime. The bridge between understanding and virtue is practice, so try out the practice after each chapter. In the conclusion, I discuss some of the ways that contemplative prayer helps us in both the short and the long term.

The Importance of Contemplative Prayer

Does prayer work? It's a fair question. Rabbi Jonathan Sacks once compared the effect of prayer on a person to tidal water rushing over a rock on a beach.[6] We cannot discern the difference the water makes on the rock in the short run. But over time, the water slowly smooths and reshapes the rock. In the long run, the rock is transformed. That is what prayer does. Over time, it smooths out our rough edges, forging us into greater alignment with the kingdom of God as we live out our days on earth.

Prayer "works" only when we consent to let God work in us. Prayer, in essence, is relational contact with the living God.

In just five verses, Luke's Gospel spells out a profound revelation (10:38–42). Mary and Martha receive Jesus into their home. Martha views her relation to Jesus in transactional terms. She is the host; Jesus is the guest. In contrast, Mary views her relation to Jesus in formational terms. She is the disciple; Jesus is the rabbi. Don't miss the profundity of this narrative. In first-century Judaism, women were seldom invited to enter into a disciple-rabbi relationship. Rather, a woman's station in life was to serve as host for the guest. Jesus doesn't rebuke Martha for choosing this posture, but when she complains to him about her sister, he replies that Mary has chosen what is better (10:42).

And what is that better station? To sit at the feet of Jesus rather than running about. In short, *being* always precedes *doing* in healthy spirituality. If *doing* for God precedes *being* with God, our faith becomes convoluted.

The Quietest Room in the World

There is a room that is completely echo-free. The Microsoft Research Lab in Redmond, Washington, houses the quietest room in the world.[7] A space smaller than a newborn's nursery, it took two full years to complete. The room is so quiet that a person can actually hear the grinding of their bones when walking inside. Field trip anybody?

Some have referred to this room as the place "where sound goes to die." It's a sound engineer's dream. The technology on the walls prevents sound waves from bouncing. I bring it up because our minds feel nothing like this—at least mine doesn't. We were created with the capacity to rid ourselves of the worries of the day by surrendering them to God. Instead, the noise inside us feels like it is constantly bouncing off the walls of our brain. The internal noise is like an echo chamber of anxiety, worry, and fear. Contemplative prayer is one of the tools we have to still the bouncing sound waves within us.

I pray that the Holy Spirit would empower you to silence the noise within. May this simple book guide you on a spiritual pilgrimage to *being with God*. And may you then access the peace, joy, compassion, and shalom that your soul relentlessly searches for.

PART 1

ABSURDITY

"ARE YOU KIDDING ME?" I blurted out.

I was staring at the computer screen when the question emerged full force. I had never before seen a goat in a tree. Have you? And the strangeness of the photo stayed with me. Goats can—and do—climb trees. Although this phenomenon seldom, if ever, occurs at the family farm in rural America, it happens every day in the coastal forests of Morocco. The next time you find yourself in Marrakesh with some time on your hands, head west eighty miles and you'll reach the Argan Forest. It is here you will find goats in the trees.

Goats in trees are an incredible metaphor for being with God. I'll get to that in a bit. But first, let's imagine ourselves in Morocco, gazing upon goats in trees. There is a reason these goats can climb. Over the course of time, their hooves developed to scale tree limbs for survival.

Perhaps you've heard of argan oil? Goats climb trees to eat the argan fruit. After their stomachs digest the fruit, the nuts are excreted out. Yep, through their bowels. Leaving no room for mis-understanding, let me be clear: the goats poop out the nuts. Oil producers then gather the excrement and pluck from the poop one argan nut at a time. Because of the digestion process, the nuts are softened, making the seeds within easier to extract. Once the seeds inside the nuts are extracted, they are then pressed into oil. The oil is collected, filtered, and sent across the ocean to a store near you so you can lather it on your hair and body. Grossed out? And yet argan oil has never been in greater demand. Surely most people aren't aware of the production process before applying argan oil to their faces.

But let's return to the main point. Moroccan goats go to great lengths for nourishment. The thought of them climbing trees may seem silly to us, but for them, it's about survival. When I first saw photos of goats in trees, it occurred to me that this image reminds me of contemplative prayer in an age of hurry, anxiety, and effi-ciency. Truthfully, the goats look ridiculous. Yet in a society where "time is money" and where the central aim is to "stay busy," the pursuit of stillness, silence, and solitude appears equally ridiculous.

The word "absurd" comes from the Latin word *sardus*, which means "deaf." "Absurdity" is the right word to describe ways of thinking, acting, and being that should not persist but nevertheless remain. Much of our lives has become absurd because we choose to remain deaf (*sardus*) to the many ways our cultural values are grinding us down, one absurd stressor at a time.

Consider the following:

Dedication to screens: absurd

Hours of lost sleep: absurd

Addiction to pornography: absurd

Poor drinking and eating habits: absurd

Keeping up with the Joneses: absurd

Lack of time to exercise and sabbath: absurd

None of these examples come as a surprise. And that is what makes them so absurd. We know these things are bad for us, yet we persist in them. And it's killing us.

Recently, my five-year-old told me from the backseat of the car that she wanted my cell phone. I asked her why, and she replied that she was bored. I told her no and then congratulated her because boredom is the gateway to imagination. She shook her head in disagreement.

A conversation with an inquirer about contemplative prayer may go something like this:

Inquirer: You just sit there?

You: Yeah, you just sit there.

Inquirer: And . . . then what happens?

You: Nothing.

Inquirer: Nothing? You just sit there?

You: Yes, we've been over this.

Sitting quietly may sound crazy, but the alternative is to stay busy. Most Americans are more comfortable with the absurdity of staying busy because it offers the illusion of progress and pro-ductivity, two of the Western world's greatest idols. Since we are on the topic of busyness, did you know the Chinese pictograph for "busy" is made of two characters? Guess what they are: *heart* and *killing*.[1] Often we believe our busyness is imparting life. Is it possible that our busyness is sometimes taking life too?

So what, then, is an alternative? I suggest that contemplative prayer is one way forward in a culture of absurdity. Let's return to the definition of contemplation offered by Robert Mulholland Jr.: "The practice of stilling ourselves before God, moving ever deeper into the core of our being and simply offering ourselves to God in totally vulnerable love."[2]

I like that definition for several reasons. First, it's simple and easy to grasp. Too often, contemplation is construed as abstract and elitist, reserved for the upper class and the overeducated. But this form of prayer is open and accessible to all people, regardless of ethnic and socioeconomic background. Second, it implies a relational connection between God and humans. We each play a part. Our part is consent, surrender, and stillness. God's part is meeting us in that posture. Third, it reminds us that we are not seeking a something but a Someone. And that Someone is a God who, above everything else, loves. There is nothing and no one to fear in contemplative prayer. We simply tune the frequency of our hearts (and minds and bodies) to a God who never stops loving us.

Contemplation is, then, one of the postures of prayer that helps us access God's love. Perhaps you're like me. I often find it hard to access God's love. Why? The problem isn't on God's end. Rather, the problem lies with me. I go too fast, move too quickly, and desire transactional (productive) spirituality over relational connection. Many Protestant churches in the West seem to be more influenced by the entertainment value of louder songs, greater platforms, and bigger programs as the standard of success than by the slow and steady rhythms of Jesus. It's no wonder people are leaving the church in droves. Many churches offer little more than what someone can experience on a leisure stroll through Times Square.

Contemplation is the reminder that *being* is always greater than *doing*. In fact, being is what best empowers doing. When we center on doing—even with the best intentions—without first resting and being, we end up weary, anxious, and prideful.

The goal of this book is to bring us back to first things:

slow down
pay attention
be still
be loved

When those practices become routine in our lives, we can do great things. Make your aim in life to be less concerned about going *fast* and more interested in going *far*. The world is in need of persevering people who are committed to the long journey of Christlikeness. This always happens, like the growth of argan fruit, over time.

But I must warn you: when we organize our lives this way, we might end up looking to many like goats in trees.

◆ PRACTICE ◆

As you begin the journey of cultivating the contemplative rhythms, let's begin with a distraction inventory. In the left column below are words that generally describe a restful state of being amid our cultural absurdity. These each correspond with a positive numeric value (+1). In the right column are words that describe a life generally in opposition to contemplative rhythms. These are each assigned a negative numeric value (-1). If you sense you are neither positive nor negative, then designate a zero to indicate that you are somewhere in between (0). At the end, total the numbers and notice whether your life at the moment is moving positively toward or negatively away from contemplative spirituality. As you evaluate each set of words, think in terms of the big picture rather than the granular details of your life. As you read through this book, decide where you need to make adjustments in order to increase being with God.

RESTFULNESS (+1)	(0)	RESTLESSNESS (-1)
Margin		Busyness
Rhythm		Hurry
Quiet		Noise

Community ·· Isolation

Solitude ··· Crowds

Delight ································· Distraction

Wonder ······························· Cynicism

Clarity ····································· Confusion

Gratitude ······································· Greed

Contentment ··························· Envy

Trust ··· Worry

Love ······································· Angst

Total: _____

WEIRD

The LORD is in his holy temple;
let all the earth be silent before him.

—Habakkuk 2:20

Our busyness can't disguise the suspicion that we are being
steadily diminished, not so much living as passing time in
a desert of our own devising.

—Kathleen Norris, *Acedia and Me*

THE WORLD was spinning quickly.

Remember life before the pandemic of 2020? The stock
market—soaring; the housing market—booming; the pace of
life—humming.

And then, for many of us, it all just kind of stopped. Or at least
it slowed down. Suffice it to say, the pandemic brought about a
great pause, and suddenly we got a glimpse of how fast-paced life
had become. The great pause imparted a revelation that our lives
up to that point had been running on equal parts adrenaline and
hurry with a healthy pinch of anxiety sprinkled on top.

Do you ever notice how deaf we become to the constant hum in our souls until we are still enough to pay attention?

But let's not get ahead of ourselves here. Permit me to take you back to an exceptionally underrated event that happened a few months before the pandemic. Go with me to the evening of July 13, 2019, at the heart of NYC tourism, Times Square.

Up until midnight, everything played out as expected. There were Broadway shows, traffic jams, full restaurants, and the sounds of joy and laughter mixed with the occasional strange shouts from that guy on the corner preaching eternal damnation. It was a usual night. And don't forget about the city lights, millions and millions of bulbs illuminating the paths of consumption and merriment.

But then, suddenly, as the evening revved up, the lights went out. For several hours, the fine people of NYC were without power. More than 72,000 people stumbled clumsily into the city's streets, creating a pathway of white glow with their cell phones. The aerial photography would later send a chill down my spine. That night, Jennifer Lopez was not amused. Neither were her fans, who had paid top dollar to watch her perform at Madison Square Garden.

Thankfully, the outage was not caused by a cyberattack or a terrorist cell. It was due to mechanical failure. But the more I thought about it, the weirder it became. In a eureka moment of clarity amid the chaos of life, I wondered aloud, "What's weirder, that the lights went out or that we expect them to always be on?"

What do you expect at 4 p.m. in Times Square? Lights.

What do you expect at 12 a.m. in Times Square? Lights.

What do you expect at 6 a.m. in Times Square? Lights.

And don't we see a similar pattern in our own lives?

We live in a society of extreme overload. The 2020 pandemic with its great pause only highlighted this truth. We learned that moderation may be at the top of the list of our forgotten virtues. We overdo good things to the point of idolatry. We binge-watch television, crush working hours, max out credit cards, and cram our calendars—all while assuming this is normal.

So if you're going to take seriously the slow and steady rhythms of Jesus—that is, the way of stillness, silence, and solitude—in this culture, you will increasingly look weird, like a goat in a tree, because the path of Christ is abnormal in a society shot through with cortisol.

Mindfulness and Contemplation

Many corporations worldwide now recognize the need for improved employee mental and emotional health. To that end, "mindfulness" has turned into a large business, with the development of apps, courses, and instructors who help people slow down and center on what matters most. In 2017, Apple named a mindfulness app, Calm, the app of the year. Many businesses designate times of the workday when employees are encouraged to create space for stillness and reflection. Some companies even employ instructors and design rooms for such activity. And some governments are spending hundreds of millions of dollars on mindfulness research, hoping that mindfulness will reduce stress and therefore lower national healthcare costs.

I celebrate this awakening in our culture, but while there are some similarities between mindfulness and Christ-centered contemplation (or contemplative prayer),[1] there are also some important differences. Both involve a focus on breath, sometimes a repetitive word or phrase, and always the invitation to slow down and calm the mind. They both release stress and help one access greater clarity. To be sure, mindfulness and Christ-centered contemplation overlap. But they are not synonymous. I see at least five main differences (generally speaking):

1. Mindfulness aims to empty one's mind; contemplation aims to fill one's mind.
2. Mindfulness centers on self-focus; contemplation centers on Spirit-focus.

3. Mindfulness helps participants get rid of their desire for harmful things; contemplation recenters participants' desire on ultimate things.
4. Mindfulness is primarily about *detachment* of ego; contemplation is primarily about *attachment* to Christ.
5. Mindfulness seeks to release; contemplation seeks to abide.

Hear me clearly: In no way am I rebuking mindfulness. I believe it to be helpful, particularly for those who want to become mentally and emotionally healthy and do not claim Christian faith. I am simply stating that mindfulness is not the same as contemplation—at least not in the way the desert fathers and mothers[2] viewed it. This is not a controversial claim. The chapters in this book will give you a clearer grasp of what the great Christian tradition means by contemplative prayer, which is a spiritual pathway that meets the felt needs of life in the modern world.

Contemplative prayer can be likened to the prodigal son returning to the arms of the father's loving embrace. This form of prayer seeks not to *achieve* anything but rather to *receive* everything. Contrasted with mindfulness, this form of prayer does not seek to empty the mind but to fill the mind with an awareness of God's presence through the indwelling of the Holy Spirit. In contemplative prayer, we do not focus on eliminating desire but instead on reordering desire in alignment with the kingdom of God. In all our running about, contemplative prayer invites us to return to the divine Triune embrace. Henri Nouwen, in his classic *The Return of the Prodigal Son*, describes the embrace like this:

> It is the place where I so much want to be, but am so fearful of being.
>
> It is the place where I will receive all I desire, all that I ever hoped for, all that I will ever need, but it is also the place where I have to let go of all I most want to hold on to.

It is the place that confronts me with the fact that truly accepting love, forgiveness, and healing is often much harder than giving it.

It is the place beyond earning, deserving, and rewarding.

It is the place of surrender and trust.[3]

Mindfulness reconnects us with ourselves. Thankfully so. But it takes us only partway down the road. Contemplation moves us beyond ourselves into the cosmic stream of eternal life. When I use the phrase "beyond ourselves," I do not mean some abstract, gnostic, pseudo-spiritual pursuit. Nor do I mean a nebulous spirituality, a system, or a philosophy. Rather, I am talking about nothing less than intimacy with the Creator, Sustainer, and Redeemer of life—the Triune God who is present in our midst. Like the prodigal son, we return to an ever-present God who waits for us in the stillness, silence, and solitude. In that place, we are received by God's loving, gracious, ever-renewing, and forgiving embrace. The presence of God is the place of surrender and trust.

In the fourth century, Basil the Great wrote a letter to his friend Gregory of Nazianzus. In it he confesses that the main stresses in life are within us; they are internal, not external. After leaving a noisy, busy, stress-filled life in the city of Cappadocia for a monastery, he had an epiphany: "I have indeed left my life in the city, but I have not yet been able to leave myself behind. We carry our indwelling disorders about with us, and so are nowhere free from the same sort of disturbances."[4]

I like this confession because it saves us from scapegoating others for the stress we carry. Basil challenges us to take responsibility for our own noise, much of which comes from within us. Sometimes the greatest stressors in life aren't caused by the external noise (e.g., your boss, your demotion, your schedule, that conflict). Sometimes the greatest stressors are caused by the internal noise we create about the external noise. I get it, burnout is real, and I am not minimizing that. Statistics report that up to 25 percent of adults are experiencing burnout at any given moment.[5] (By the way, burnout is not restricted to the workforce. Homemakers can feel it just as acutely.) But I can attest from experience that the way I internally choose to handle the external strains and stresses of life affects my well-being. We can choose how we will allow things beyond our control to impact us. And our lives depend on choosing wisely.

If you find yourself a touch leery of contemplative prayer because it sounds too mystical and fear it could lead you away from devotion to Christ, consider the encouraging words of Rowan Williams, former archbishop of the Church of England. Williams, who is thoroughly orthodox, challenged church leadership on the matter in a speech:

> Contemplation is very far from being just one kind of thing that Christians do: it is the key to prayer, liturgy, art and ethics, the key to the essence of a renewed humanity that is capable of seeing the world and other subjects in the world with freedom—freedom from self-oriented, acquisitive habits and the distorted understanding that comes from them. To put it boldly, contemplation is the only ultimate answer to the unreal and insane world that our financial systems and our advertising culture and our chaotic and unexamined emotions encourage us to inhabit. To learn contemplative practice is to learn what we need so as to live truthfully and honestly and lovingly. It is a deeply revolutionary matter.[6]

Williams's belief that contemplation is the key to prayer, art, and ethics is striking. Many Christians treat prayer in general as optional and are often unaware of contemplative prayer. Philosopher and author James K. A. Smith once remarked to me that "one of the most important practices the church must take up in its gatherings is silence." I think he's correct. Habakkuk prophesied, "The LORD is in his holy temple; let all the earth be silent before him" (2:20). Because the New Testament declares that we, the body of Christ, have become God's temple, we must take seriously our commitment to steward the presence of God within. Contemplative prayer is one way we can do this. That this form of prayer has been elusive in the Western church is a tragedy. So many of our spiritual ancestors were committed to this pathway of following Jesus. Maybe we should follow their lead—as they followed Christ.

◆ PRACTICE ◆

Start small. Before launching into the day's activities and responsibilities, commit to being quiet to start the day. Perhaps that means you need to wake up ten minutes earlier before the kids or to create space before heading off to work or school. No matter the circumstance, set a timer for five to seven minutes, during which you can take time to pause before the rush of the day and still the noise within you. Consider taking a notepad and pen into this time so that you can jot down things that come up that you'd like to remember when the time is over.

Later we will integrate praying Scripture and connecting words and phrases to breathing. But for now, begin by just being quiet and taking notice of what comes up.

TECH

LORD, our Lord,
   how majestic is your name in all the earth!
You have set your glory
   in the heavens. . . .
When I consider your heavens,
   the work of your fingers,
the moon and the stars,
   which you have set in place,
what is mankind that you are mindful of them,
   human beings that you care for them? . . .
LORD, our Lord,
   how majestic is your name in all the earth!
                                   —Psalm 8:1, 3–4, 9

We flee from boredom because of what we encounter there, namely, ourselves.

                        —David Foster Wallace, *The Pale King*

Doljanchi

In South Korea, some parents and caregivers still practice an ancient and fascinating tradition with their crawling babies. *Doljanchi* is a lighthearted fortune-telling exercise that no one takes too seriously but is entertaining nonetheless. For Americans, it's something similar to opening a fortune cookie after eating cashew chicken at your local Chinese restaurant.

In *doljanchi*, a family gathers in a room and places the baby on the floor. On the opposite end of the room lie several objects—for example, an apple, a coin, a book, and a paintbrush.[1] The adults encourage the baby to crawl to the objects, and whichever object the baby first picks up provides a forecast of the child's destiny. If the apple is selected, then perhaps the baby will never go hungry. If the coin, perhaps wealth is in the baby's future. The book might mean a future academic. And the paintbrush might signify creativity.

In *The Influential Mind*, Tali Sharot details her *doljanchi* experience when practicing the tradition with her baby. The family gathered, the objects were strewn about the floor, and with eager pace the baby began her crawl. Only something strange happened next. While the child was aligned to go straight toward the objects, she suddenly took a hard, left turn and headed toward an adjacent coffee table, where a cell phone lay on its surface. The baby reached up for the cell phone, showcasing to all what her future might hold.

The significance for Sharot is that "we are born with an automatic predisposition to learn from those around us."[2] Therefore, if parents and caregivers model an addiction to digital technology in front of their children, they are almost guaranteeing that their children will grow up to share the same addiction. My wife and I find ourselves in constant tension with our use of technology and how we are modeling appropriate usage for our daughter. I often feel that we fail to set the best example.

Hasta La Vista, Baby

I am not anti-tech, but I do have concerns about where technology is going—and where a not-insignificant portion of the world's population appears more than willing to be led. It seems self-evident to me that much of our use of technology today is in service of amusing ourselves to death, as Neil Postman famously put it.[3] Technology is, for many, an escape from life's hard questions and incessant demands. We are a society in crisis, longing for renewal but settling for relief. Author John Eldredge exposes our temptation to short-term relief in the form of checking out, numbing and sedating ourselves through the false gods of television, social media, unhealthy foods, and alcohol.[4] What we really desire is long-term renewal that satisfies the soul and not merely appetite. If the Netflix documentary *The Social Dilemma* is correct, then we have been duped into believing that current technological trends will lead to happier, healthier lives. I suggest that our obsession with technology today is one of the greatest threats to being with God. After all, who wants to be with God when we can be entertained by ourselves?

In 1991, *Terminator 2: Judgment Day* came to theaters everywhere west of the Middle East. I was a ten-year-old punk kid pranking my way through third grade in Nashville. For months, the sci-fi thriller plot dominated the dialogue between me and my elementary school classmates. We all feared the day when the robots would overtake the humans.

I am not sure that fear has ever gone away. Yet these days I like to shift the angle of the conversation when the topic presents itself, as it often does. As technology continues to advance, I am less concerned that robots are becoming like humans and more concerned that humans are becoming like robots. And all this has tremendous effects on the spiritual life.

Maybe the movie *Inception* got it right. Perhaps we are being "programmed" by forces behind the scenes that manipulate our behavior. And the illusion is that we believe we are free agents, acting from our own original impulses.

I am not convinced that the rise in video gaming is good for our children's imaginations or abilities to relationally connect. I am not convinced that social media improves our chances to combat relentless anxiety and self-doubt. I am not convinced that checking email before I even get out of bed is good for my mental health. I am not convinced that 5G is really about increased internet speed as much as it is about storing information to induce consumers to act in ways that will increase profits for big businesses. If Google gets its way, we will all be wearing augmented reality glasses to filter our every move.

Again, I am not a Luddite. But I do have concerns.

I imagine many of us in our highly connected, always-on culture as tiny rocks, skimming across the water, moving with such frenetic velocity that we touch only the surface of life. The consequence of this is that we rarely pause long enough to immerse into the deep. The slowing of life is what permits us to sink deeply enough to truly live. Instead, we typically settle for skimming our way through existence. Maybe this explains why Jesus frequently employed agricultural imagery in his teachings. Farming takes time. It's not efficient. But it is effective.

Some may point out that, as a first-century Jew, Jesus lived in an agricultural context. But nearby cities used advanced technology that also would have been common to the people of Galilee. Yet Jesus rarely spoke the language of urban industry. Time and again, he illustrated his wisdom with the language of farming: the coming harvest, the seeds of renewal, and so forth.

Perhaps farming captures something true about human life that the efficiency of industry can't. The Industrial Revolution of the 1800s taught us to demand efficiency, assert control, and boast self-reliance. Contrast that with the ancient way of Jesus, who invites us to slow our pace, surrender control, and submit to the freedom of interdependence. Maybe it takes time to become whole. Maybe it takes time to cultivate the fruit of God's Spirit. And if we learn the slow and effective rhythms of Jesus, we can better descend into the depths of his way and become the kinds of people who reflect the kingdom of heaven on earth.

Let's take this further. If the 1800s inspired us to view life through the *industrial* lens, the 2000s invite us to view life through the *technological* lens.

Father Martin Bernhard, a monk from the Norcia monastery, offers a warning to the Western world: "When the light in most people's faces comes from the glow of the laptop, the smartphone, or the television screen, we are living in a Dark Age."[5]

In his book *Free to Focus*, Michael Hyatt reveals disturbing research about Americans' email habits. In a study commissioned by the software company Adobe, 80 percent of US workers checked email before arriving at work, then spent more than six hours per day sending emails. And 30 percent of these workers checked their email account(s) before getting out of bed. Another study revealed that almost 40 percent of respondents checked email after 11 p.m. and that 75 percent engaged with work email on the weekends. This time added up to more than seventy hours of work per week.[6]

Filling in the Cracks

On top of email, add our obsession with social media, twenty-four-hour news coverage, pervasive gaming, and other forms of passive entertainment, and it becomes apparent that we are technologically obsessed. Tech isn't all bad. But no one in their right mind would say it's all good either. James K. A. Smith said it well: "We carry in our pockets the possibility of unceasing jolts of novelty."[7] Screens of luminescence; screens of omnipresence. The core problem is not that we possess technology but that we permit technology to possess us.

In the 1960s, people believed that, thanks to technology, we'd eventually have so much leisure time that we wouldn't know how to spend it. Many even predicted that our long-extended vacations would be insufferable. Quite the opposite has happened. With all our new tech, we have found more reasons both to work long hours and to waste our lives filling in the cracks in search of snippets of useless information. Author David Zahl wonders if our "screens distract us from our core pain, which is the pain of not being enough, the reality of our finitude, what some call existential angst."[8] When we refuse to be still and know that God is God (Ps. 46:10) and must fill every open sliver of time with the pursuit of amusement, we must ask ourselves, "Am I in search of something 'out there' that is already available to me 'in here'?" Do we trust that the identity-giving God who lives within us is more satisfying than the insatiable pursuit of endless distractions?

A significant amount of time is now spent in search of wall outlets. Anyone delayed at an airport can plainly view this phenomenon. With our devices comes the promise of constant connection with the external world. But with this promise also comes the price of constant disconnection from our internal self, where, by the way, the Holy Spirit indwells and awaits our attention.

Albert Einstein—maybe you've heard of him—once pondered,

> Our time is distinguished by wonderful achievements in the fields of scientific understanding and the technical application of those insights. Who would not be cheered by this? But let us not forget that knowledge and skills alone cannot lead humanity to a happy and dignified life. Humanity has every reason to place the proclaimers of high moral standards and values above the discoverers of objective truth. What humanity owes to personalities like Buddha, Moses, and Jesus ranks for me higher than all the achievements of the inquiring and constructive mind.[9]

Although God gave humans the minds and ingenuity to invent the iPhone and other modern technologies, God gives us something greater. Jesus invites us and empowers us to discover a better way that restores us to God's full intent for our lives. Jesus frequently taught his disciples how to disengage from society so that they might reengage with something (or rather Someone) transformative. Part 2 of this book reveals how that happens. Contemplative prayer isn't about leaving anything. It's about being filled with God's Spirit, increasing our self-awareness, and becoming available to others from a place of resource and depth.

In 1969 and 1970, Johns Hopkins University and the Brookings Institution hosted a slew of conferences on the impact of information technology. At this point, the internet was more than a decade away from being invented. Yet Herbert Simon, professor of computer science and psychology at Carnegie Mellon, warned of the immense burden that would arise with the growth of information, stating, "Information consumes the attention of its recipients . . . and a wealth of information creates a poverty of attention."[10]

Did you catch that? *A wealth of information creates a poverty of attention.* Could a sentence better describe what is happening in this age? Information is ubiquitous, but human attention is scattered. We are confronted with a sea of options. We are afraid we are going to miss out, yet we never really experience anything deeply. We are rocks skimming across the surface of the water.

Technology is not the enemy. But the way in which we have surrendered to technology's omnipresence is troublesome. Technology carries the promise of being constantly informed—and I like to be informed as much as anybody—but it is possible to be both informed and malformed. Being informed is not the same as being transformed. The healthiest humans I know value transformation over information—and know how to use information in a way that cultivates wisdom. Our society frantically chases information to the neglect of formation. This is the spirit of the age.

I am not anti-technology. But I do have concerns. And maybe you do too.

◆ PRACTICE ◆

Anglican priest Samuel Wells offers a simple challenge: "If a small electrical device owns you, begin the day with a sacred time of refraining from reaching for it; have a whole day a week without being at its behest; identify conversations and moments it is never allowed to interrupt."[11]

As you engage in more of the contemplative and reflective journey, consider one or all of the following practices for the next seven days.

1. Refuse to pull out your phone when you wait in line this week. Instead, notice the life happening around you. See the people, smell the atmosphere, breathe in deeply, and ask God how you can pray for what is occurring before your eyes.

2. Do not drive with your phone in reach. Place your phone somewhere out of arm's reach and keep your eyes on the road—where they belong. At a traffic light, refuse to check email or social media. Don't worry if you don't have access to your music library. Drive in silence for a change, using the silence to be with God.

3. Keep track of how often you stare at screens when children, your spouse, or friends are in the room. There are apps that provide intel as to how long you spend on your phone. You can also determine ahead of time when you will and will not watch television.

HEAR

Hear, O Israel: The LORD our God, the LORD is one.

—Deuteronomy 6:4

About 30 million people in the United States are exposed to
hazardous sound levels at their workplace every day.

—Ron Chepesiuk, "Decibel Hell: The Effects
of Living in a Noisy World"

LIVING IN A CITY has advantages; low blood pressure is
not among them. For people who live in urban areas, one of the
contributing factors to rising blood pressure is noise exposure.
Exposure to loud noise may also lead to heart disease, sleep disturbances, and stress.[1] Pervasive noise works on our souls in ways that
lie beneath our awareness. If sounds were made visible, we would
observe what might look like garbage everywhere.

Given the volume of ambient noise, maybe this is the most
crucial time to take seriously Deuteronomy 6:4: "Hear, O Israel:
The LORD our God, the LORD is one." But how can we hear the
God of heaven when we are immersed in such a racket on earth?

The Hebrew word for "hear" is *shema*. It means "to perceive, under-stand, and listen to." If God is speaking, as the Scriptures suggest he is, do you perceive it? Amid the noise, how can we understand him? Are there spiritual strategies that can help us cut through the clamor to hear words of life?

New York, I Love You

Elaina and I moved to Manhattan in 2011. At that stage in our marriage, it was just the two of us. Living in a quaint downtown neighborhood, we experienced daily access to culture, coffee, and creativity in ministry. We were immersed in young adult flourish-ing. And because we were having the time of our lives, we were largely oblivious to the noise around us. Furthermore, for me, the sounds of the city were inspiring. The car horns, power drills, and street chatter weren't a personal nuisance but rather signs of cul-tural progress. With every jackhammer in use, the allure of the city became more electric with potential. We were flourishing. New York, I love you.

It wasn't until our daughter was born in 2013 that I heard those sounds differently and started to notice how annoyingly loud the city can be. I remember our first "Daddy stroll" when I wheeled my newborn up and down the streets of our neighborhood. Ex-posing her newborn ears to loud noise pollution made me sick to my stomach. Upon arriving back at our apartment, I researched "noise cancelling headphones for newborns." Later, I would learn that being exposed to noise can affect a child's developing brain. Stress hormones are released when people experience constant noise pollution, and this in turn affects psychological well-being. This means we might well be raising the next generation with an increased risk of mental illness. A recent study revealed that "many children who live near noisy airports or streets have been found to suffer from stress and other problems, such as impair-ments in memory, attention level, and reading skill."[2] Despite feeble attempts to regulate noise levels with neighborhood signs that read, "DON'T HONK, $350 PENALTY," law enforcement can do little to enforce noise restrictions.

We love New York City, and there are many advantages to raising children in a metropolitan area. But we decided it was time to pray about raising our daughter in a different context.

Sounds of the City

Did you know that the leading cause of deafness today is not old age but exposure to noise?[3] Now maybe you're thinking, *I live in a rural context*, or *I live in the suburbs*, or *My city is not as loud as New York City*. But think about this: according to the United Nations, by the year 2050, two-thirds of the world's population will live in urban areas.[4] And no matter where you currently live, over thirty million people in the United States are exposed to hazardous sound levels at their workplace every day.[5] Of the top seven noisiest cities on earth, three are reportedly in the United States (New York, Los Angeles, and San Francisco).[6] I now live in a sleepy neighborhood outside Charleston, South Carolina, but as I write this chapter, I can hear the pervasive beeping sounds of trucks in reverse. Noise is inescapable.

Sound is measured in decibels (dB). A healthy exposure level should not exceed 85 dB, unless necessary and infrequent. After 85 decibels, sound becomes damaging to the ears. To put this into perspective, here are some sounds humans are exposed to throughout an ordinary day:

Alarm clock: 80 dB (your day begins just below the threatening noise level!)

Morning conversation: 65 dB

Busy traffic: 95 dB

Car horn at a stoplight: 119 dB

Jackhammer: 130 dB

Siren on the interstate: 140 dB

Office noise: 40 dB

Neighbor mowing the lawn: 86 dB

Same neighbor leaf blowing: 105 dB

Evening rock concert: 120 dB

Think about this: At many sporting events, an artificial dB meter is displayed on the jumbo screen encouraging increased levels of noise from fans. That's kind of crazy. It seems we are unaware of the audio trash we put in our ears. Not to be a curmudgeon, but whatever team you root for, sacrificing your hearing health is not worth it. And to the annoying guy sitting behind you who whistles with two fingers in his mouth: (1) that's gross, and (2) that whistle gets up to 116 dB. For the sake of us all, please stop. Besides, your whistle has zero impact on the outcome of the game.

Let me drop some algorithmic knowledge on you. Going from 50 dB to 100 dB isn't twice as loud. It is sixteen times as loud. The decibel scale isn't linear. The impact compounds as the noise level increases. This aural pollution burrows its way into the grooves of your life. The legal world is beginning to recognize the impact of noise on health. In Japan, one court awarded over $7 million to people living near an air base in western Tokyo as compensation for aircraft noise, but it rejected their demand to restrict flight operations at the base.[7]

Evangelical churches seldom encourage forms of worship that foster stillness and silence. Some churches now even provide protective ear wear because the decibel level of their worship music can be damaging.

This constant noise is taking a toll on the animal kingdom as well. For example, studies show that loud sounds "cause caterpillars' hearts to beat faster and bluebirds to have fewer chicks. Animals use sound for a variety of reasons, including to navigate, find food, attract mates, and avoid predators."[8] For animals, noise pollution can affect their ability to both thrive and survive.

So far, every example I've provided is above sea level. Let's go below.

Under the Sea

In Disney's 1988 classic *The Little Mermaid*, Sebastian, the Jamaican-accented crab, breaks into melodic celebration, singing, "Darling, it's better down where it's wetter." But I'm not convinced he would sing that today. Due to global trade, sonar, and oil drilling, among other things, the decibel level of life under the sea has risen.

Recently, *National Geographic* reported, "Increasing noise is [causing] . . . a growing problem for those that live in the ocean. Ships, oil drills, sonar devices, and seismic tests have made the once tranquil marine environment loud and chaotic. Whales and dolphins are particularly impacted by noise pollution. These marine mammals rely on echolocation to communicate, navigate, feed, and find mates, and excess noise interferes with their ability to effectively echolocate." Naval sonar devices "can be as loud as 235 decibels and travel hundreds of miles under water, interfering with whales' ability to use echolocation. . . . Sonar can cause mass strandings of whales on beaches and alter the feeding behavior. . . . Ships looking for deep-sea oil or gas deposits tow devices called air guns and shoot pulses of sound down to the ocean floor. The sound blasts can damage the ears of marine animals and cause serious injury."[9]

In the early 1990s, researchers at the National Oceanic Atmospheric Administration played low-frequency sounds in Antarctica that were picked up halfway around the world in Bermuda. Imagine what an ocean liner, importing your recent online toothbrush purchase from Asia, sounds like underwater.[10] Humans are increasing noise levels to the point of absurdity, even under the sea.

Given the noise pollution under the sea, I wonder what kinds of stress hormones are being released into sea creatures. Poor Sebastian. These are the same sea creatures we eat. Poor us.

Quieting the Noise

The last fifty years of human history have seen more change than the previous five thousand years combined. The acceleration of travel, communication, technology, and pace of life substantiates that claim. Our lives are getting "noisier" in every conceivable category, including religion. The late pastor Eugene Peterson said, "American religion is conspicuous for its messianically pretentious energy, its embarrassingly banal prose, and its impatiently hustling ambition. None of these marks is remotely biblical. None is faintly in evidence in the gospel story. All of them are thoroughly documented diseases of the spirit."[11]

Like never before, we have more information within reach, yet less time and attention to translate information into wisdom. Theologian Thomas Oden wrote, "The gains of modern life have been accompanied by the loss of wonder. The achievements of the end of the previous millennium have left us with a deep sense of rootlessness and moral confusion."[12] Many of us find ourselves exerting energy in a thousand different directions, and over the course of a life, this adds up to one big waste of time. You might even say we suffer from what writer Linda Stone calls "continuous partial attention."[13] This means that we have to cultivate time and attention today, or intimacy with God simply won't happen. Quieting the noise to be with God has to be an intentional choice. It will definitely render us odd creatures. You might even say we will become to the world like goats in the trees.

◆ PRACTICE ◆

The most central passage in all of Scripture is Deuteronomy 6:4. The writer invites us to hear: "Hear, O Israel: The LORD our God, the LORD is one."

When you quiet yourself, whose voice do you hear? Perhaps it's your inner critic, or your parent/caregiver, or your boss. It is not uncommon to hear these voices first. Some of these voices have been traumatically embedded in our neural pathways. To gain freedom from these loudest voices, we must retrain our minds to hear God's words from Scripture. Do you permit Scripture to speak into your life each day? Decide whether it is time to let in more of God's voice through the sacred text and what that might look like in a habituated practice.

Each day I follow the Anglican practice of Scripture reading called "the daily office" by reading the passages selected from four parts of the Bible: Psalms, Old Testament, New Testament, and Gospel. Together, they provide a well-balanced scriptural diet to digest before being still before God. You can find these daily passages online through a simple web search. Consider what scriptural rhythm would be helpful for you during this season of life.

PART 2

NECESSITY

In the award-winning 2013 film *Gravity*, earth is portrayed as noisy, busy, and full of agendas, while space is depicted as a silent and timeless void. The film's climax occurs about halfway through. On the precipice of death, Dr. Ryan Stone, played by Sandra Bullock, utters an unforgettable and bone-chilling confession: "I'd pray, but no one ever taught me how."

Boom. Like a cannonball hurtling through the air, the truth of her confession targets the very foundations of Western Christianity. Many churchgoing Christians, even those who profess a deep spirituality, secretly feel incompetent when it comes to prayer. To borrow a phrase from the New Testament, "My brothers and sisters, this should not be" (James 3:10). It really can't be, in fact. There is no such thing as a dynamic spirituality without a healthy prayer life. I repeat—with mercy and grace—there is no such thing as a dynamic spirituality without a healthy prayer life.

Spirituality is synonymous with divine intimacy. Spirituality is nothing less than intimacy with God through prayer. Prayer *is* the spiritual life. Without prayer, there is no spiritual life.

When Dr. Stone faces the probability of death and sorrowfully confesses that no one ever taught her to pray, she is indirectly confessing that she was not given the tools to develop a spiritual life. The foundation of spirituality does not derive from reading books, attending church, or learning Christian lingo. It comes from time spent in contact with the living God through prayer. To pray is to entangle oneself with the divine. Without prayer, we are merely present to ourselves. To be present to oneself is not a bad thing; it's just not spirituality.

This section of the book aims to help you avoid the confession Dr. Stone made. Contemplative prayer is not easy, particularly when we have been thoroughly shaped by a culture of absurdity. So let's jump into the waters together and discover the intimacy of being with God.

NOISE

But the LORD was not in the wind. After the wind there was an earthquake, but the LORD was not in the earthquake. After the earthquake came a fire, but the LORD was not in the fire. And after the fire came a gentle whisper.

—1 Kings 19:11–12

[Like] a donkey going round and round in a mill, the mind cannot step out of the circle to which it is tethered.

—St. Hesychios, *On Watchfulness and Holiness* (eighth century)

MANHATTAN IS THE CITY where noise refuses to sleep. Sirens are the soundtrack. Every evening, Tenth Avenue jams with irritated drivers lining up to enter the thin gates of the Lincoln Tunnel. When I lived there, their aggravated negotiations sent an unwelcome, perpetual cacophony of horns through my living room windows. This symphony sounded more like a middle school band than a municipal orchestra.

Bordering our apartment was a park called the Highline, where neighbors and visitors strolled along speaking every language imaginable. Manhattan is like a modern-day Babel, only with many towers and equally as many tongues. After two years in the city, my wife and I welcomed a baby girl into our family, who—sweetly but loudly—voiced her needs around the clock. In sum, the sheer decibel levels of life can rise high.

New York City has long been known for the clamor of its streets, but as revealed in the previous chapter, research supports that noise pollution is on the rise. A study showed that in 1968 it took fifteen hours to record one hour of pure nature sounds without the ambient sounds of airplanes, cars, and other manufactured items. In 2005, it took more than two thousand hours of recorded time to yield the same hour of pure nature sounds.[1] As more and more of the world's population moves to cities, our lives are not wanting for noise.

The tragedy in all of this is that our prayers often imitate the noise of the city. If you are like me, your prayers can be dominated by talking at God and speaking to God to the neglect of being with God. And when I run out of things to say or things to think, it's time to move on to the next item on the day's schedule. I'm imagining what my wife would think if this were the extent of my conversation with her. I would render her voice mute. I would reduce our relationship to a monologue, and that's not much of a relationship. Many outwardly boast of a robust prayer life but inwardly are anxious, chatty, and bored.

Savoring the Moment

We all live out of value systems. Even rejecting value systems is a value system of rejecting value systems. Whether or not we are aware of our values (conscious or subconscious), we all have values and make life decisions based on them. My values may be best arranged in the following order: faith, family, and ramen.

I'm sort of serious. When visiting a new place, I search ahead of time to locate the best ramen noodle shop that context has to offer. Now, when I mention the word "ramen," some of you are imagining the ten-cent packages of ramen in your local grocery store. Let the record state that those ramen imposters are *not* what I am referring to. They are unhealthy counterfeits, silly imitations of the real deal. I'm talking about robust Tonkotsu ramen with rich, homemade broth, pork belly, and a soft-boiled egg, garnished with seaweed and the works. This kind of culinary art you'll find only in an authentic Japanese restaurant. It's a game changer.

Several years ago, I was invited to speak on the Enneagram and spiritual formation at a church in Queens. I flew in to New York a day early just to visit one of the most authentic ramen shops in the United States. In the neighborhood of Williamsburg, Ichiran is a bucket-list restaurant for ramen lovers. Upward of $30 per bowl, the experience is worth every penny. And that experience sheds light on the topic of being with God.

Immediately upon entering the restaurant, you are handed a number and escorted to an enclosed cubicle, where you will stand—not sit—alone for the meal. It's sort of like a voting booth dining experience. As you slurp the noodle-y goodness, the solitude enhances your ability to savor every bite.

Historically, ramen was the poor man's lunch, and the idea was for factory workers to eat quickly and talk seldom so that they could get back to their jobs efficiently on a full stomach.

But unlike the ramen of history, my solitary meal was not about efficiency but about delight. Devoid of the presence of other people, conversations, and visual distractions (none of which are typically bad things), the experience allowed me to channel all my focus and senses into one object of desire: ramen.

For thirty minutes, I took my time and savored each bite. Then I left gratified. I realized that nothing in my life is like that. When sharing meals with the ones we love, how often are our phones on the table? When enjoying conversation with a dear friend, how easy is it to look over their shoulder to see who entered the room? When playing with your child, how easy is it to be distracted and to mentally drift back into work drama? When reading Scripture, how often do we wander onto our phones?

The enemy seduces us most when we live noisy, distracted, and hurried lives. Research shows we are now interrupted or distracted about every three minutes.[2] This means that in the course of any given day, we are distracted more than 320 times. I think that estimate is low given the omnipresence of technology.

It's becoming a rare thing to be fully in one place—mind, body, and spirit. We, like the horcruxes in Harry Potter, are split and scattered in a thousand directions. The noise of life splinters our attention and robs us of the present moment.

Seeking the Silence

I'm not suggesting that noise is always bad. The Psalms invite us to *shout* to the Lord with song and instrument to destroy the idols around us. In Exodus, the Israelites marched (stomped, really) around Jericho, blew trumpets, and shouted mightily to destroy the walls of that wicked city (Exod. 6). Noise can serve a redemptive purpose; it can be used, as the Israelites showed, to deconstruct evil. But it is silence that has the power to reconstruct. And we need this kind of reconstruction every day because all too often our lives are full of noise.

In the early eighteenth century, Madame Jeanne-Marie Guyon, a mystic from France, wrote about the revolution of silence in her prayer life. She longed to see those young in faith "make a transition from anxious striving to stillness and pure trust in God."[3] Her instruction was to cultivate a prayer life that was far more passive than active, more still than busy, and more listening than speaking.

Now, before you think I view prayer as one big, silent sit, let me repeat that we do, in fact, need to talk, think, petition, and confess as part of our prayer life. These types of prayer—which reign supreme in the Western church—are a part of cataphatic spirituality (meaning to engage the senses). But my assumption is that you are already proficient in these forms of prayer. So rather than reinforcing what you already do well, I hope to plant a seed in your soul that being with God is perhaps the missing dimension in your prayer life.

How do we go about seeking silence with God amid all the noise? Must we leave the city, take a vacation, hire a sitter, or retreat to a monastery every time we desire to pray this way? Martin Laird, professor of theology at Villanova University, asserts that a sound-proof environment isn't a prerequisite for silent prayer. In fact, he explains that fixating on noise often only creates more noise in our thinking:

> Coping with disruptive noise that we simply cannot do anything about does not so much call for praying [for] noise reduction as for being resolved that it's okay for the noise to be there if nothing can be done about it. To get caught up in a buzzing commentary on how irritating the noise is makes for a noisy relationship with noise.... First, we are in a position to learn something from silence and its generous way of allowing noise to be present when it happens to be present. To get caught up in commentary on the noise will not make it go away but will only tighten the clenching of our jaws around our preference that the noise be gone. Silence is wide and gracious enough to allow sound, even irritating sound, to be present. Second, instead of trying to push disruption away, we shift our attention away from the disrupting noise to our prayer word or to whatever our contemplative practice is.[4]

Getting hung up on the presence of noise is one of many ways the inner noise of the mind can be just as loud as the sirens on the street, and shaking this inner noise will require more than taking a train ride out into the country. The practice of contemplative prayer teaches us to silence noise no matter the context. It begins with "nothing more than to meet the noise with stillness and not commentary."[5] Our inner commentary adds to the noise from which we are seeking freedom.

Inner Noise

When the coronavirus pandemic swept around the globe in 2020, life slowed down in many places for a specified period of time. I remember wondering if this was perhaps a great reset that the world needed to slow the pace and quiet the noise. What I discovered was that even when the external noise was quieted (e.g., work, traffic, schedules), the internal noise revved just as loudly—if not louder—in the form of anxiety, fear, and incessant inner monologues.

Psychologist, author, and science journalist Daniel Goleman contends that "there are two main varieties of distractions: sensory and emotional."[6] Having dealt with the external, sensory distractions above, we now turn to the emotional, internal noise within.

Years ago, aware of the inner noise of my mind, I spent a day at a nearby monastery. I had diagnosed the problem of noise (both outer and inner) but had yet to learn the skill of silence. Arriving early on a cold January morning, I sat patiently and expectantly in the sanctuary as the monks in their monastic robes chanted in unison. They completed their sunrise service and slowly vacated the space. The room was silent and still, yet I found the inner chatter of my mind deafening. I had come for peace, but after two hours, I was only more aware of the war in my mind. Dejected, I got up and left. I simply had no idea how to silence the inner monologue. I felt powerless, inept, and spiritually immature in my relationship with God.

Soon after, I stumbled upon the wisdom of St. Hesychios (from the eighth century), who said, "[Like] a donkey going round and round in a mill, the mind cannot step out of the circle to which it is tethered."[7] Even when the outer noise is muted, the inner chatter continues. Three chief triggers perpetuate this cycle:

Compare, Control, Consume

When we are still, it is embarrassing how insecure we tend to become as we compare ourselves to others. We obsess over questions like the following:

Am I good enough?
Are they better/smarter/more influential than me?

In the absence of noise, our minds consciously and subconsciously attempt to control circumstances around us:

Is my future secure?
How might I achieve my desired outcome?

When the external sounds around us fade, we consume media to fill in the gaps, justifying:

I only binge-watch because I can't stand my work.
I'm not on my phone that much.

These conversations dominate the mind and consume emotional and mental energy.

It's humbling when we discover that we are not creating our thoughts as much as our thoughts are creating us. And like a donkey, we go round and round, unable to escape the mill. In the end, the aphorism rings true: the mind is a wonderful servant and a terrible master. Laird again contends:

> In early seasons of practice . . . when we try to be silent we find that there is anything but silence. This inner noise is generated by a deeply ingrained tendency, reinforced over a lifetime, to derive our sense of who we are and what our life is about from these thoughts and feelings. We look within and genuinely think that we are our thoughts and feelings. If our thoughts and feelings were a mass of vines and branches, we would say we were smack

in the middle of it all. In fact, we might even say that we were this tangle of vines.[8]

Thinking is a wonderful thing. I try to think daily. But we must also make space for the pursuit of God beyond the bounds of critical reasoning. At the monastery, this much became clear: tragically, my mind was determining the script of my heart, soul, and will—and I had little control over it. I needed balance; I needed breakthrough. Only months later did I discover that many of our spiritual ancestors understood this and developed tools to help them move deeply into silence; and in the silence, God met them. They learned the lost art of being with God. As we seek to learn the lost art of being with God, we need to take seriously the words of Dietrich Bonhoeffer: "We are silent early in the morning because God should have the first word, and we are silent before going to bed because the last word also belongs to God."[9]

◆ PRACTICE ◆

This week pay close attention to the first place your mind veers when you wake up (e.g., email, anxiety, Scripture, finances, a relationship). These initial directions often reveal from where you draw your identity.

Let's begin the practice of seeking God in the silence in the shallow end of the pool. Resist the temptation to dive too deeply too quickly. Beginners are often tempted to prematurely jettison the path due to frustration, perceiving a lack of results. But learning contemplative prayer is like starting a new exercise program—you have to learn to use new muscles, which always feels awkward and unproductive at first.

In the sixth century, Benedict of Nursia developed a meditative approach to Scripture reading called *lectio divina* (Latin for "divine reading"). This method prioritizes what God is speaking to us. Through *lectio divina*, we invite the Holy Spirit into the reading as we move in four distinct directions: read, meditate, pray, contemplate. Since these terms may not be familiar to you, I've replaced them with *read*, *reflect*, *write*, and *rest* in the exercise below. Follow this simple pathway in your Scripture reading today.

1. Create an inviting/inspiring space. Perhaps this means lighting a candle, tidying a room, or sitting in your favorite chair.
2. Select a passage to read from Scripture.
3. Have paper/journal and a pen handy.
4. Give yourself to these four directions (five minutes for each):
   - Read—Slowly read the selected text three times.
   - Reflect—Select a word or phrase that stands out to you.
   - Write—Spend time writing about why you selected that word or phrase.
   - Rest—Suspend all thought and sit quietly with God. Trust that God knows your worry, anxiety, and longings and is acting on your behalf (Rom. 8:28).

ROOM

But when you pray, go into your room, close the door and pray to your Father, who is unseen. Then your Father, who sees what is done in secret, will reward you.

—Matthew 6:6

Find the door of your heart, you will discover it is the door of the kingdom of God.

—John Chrysostom, in Anthony Bloom, *Beginning to Pray*

WHILE YOU ARE CHECKING EMAIL on your laptop, a friend approaches you and launches into a story. Meanwhile, your phone is on the table, and your newly purchased smartwatch is fixed around your wrist. A text message comes in, and as your friend goes on, your computer, watch, and phone all ding to alert you. In this one moment, you are attempting to check email, listen to a friend, and read a text message that has been delivered to three devices at once. It's easy to imagine this scenario because it's become a normal experience in everyday life.

We tolerate a life of distraction. Nay, we *invite* a life of distraction because we think it makes us more productive. We make ourselves endlessly available for any and every intrusion, scattering attention in several directions at once. Notifications, pop-ups, and disturbances invade our brain space. I'm just as guilty as anyone. When we divide our attention in this way, we are never fully present to any one thing in life. Deep within, we know this is true, but often we lack the discipline to do anything about it.

The beloved priest and writer Henri Nouwen knew this struggle all too well. He redefined discipline as "the effort to create space"[1] in order to notice God. In other words, we must create room in our lives if we are to live deeply, truly, and beautifully with God. Instead, we often arrange life in such a way that all free space is taken up by endless intrusions.

Pastor and author Charles Stone did the math for us: if we were to reclaim just two hours every day to focus deeply on one thing at a time, we would have an extra month each year of concentrated attention.[2] The fruit of this habit would be astounding in our lives. In Matthew 5, Jesus addresses this. In the greatest sermon ever told, Jesus breaks down authentic spirituality into three central practices: give, pray, fast. Volumes have been written on each practice. For the purposes of this book, Jesus's instruction on prayer warrants our attention. Not only does Jesus guide the disciples in *how* to pray (this is what Christians refer to as the Lord's Prayer), but he also tells them *where* to pray: "But when you pray, go into your room, close the door and pray to your Father, who is unseen" (Matt. 6:6).

The Jewish ritual system gathered the people to pray in the synagogue three times per day. Jesus never renounced this practice, but he did advocate also cultivating a private prayer life. Notice in this Scripture passage that Jesus assumes his disciples will pray. He doesn't say "if" you pray but "when." In addition, he says he wants his followers to pray in secret.

It is tempting to rely on public worship services and to neglect personal intimacy with God. In the Sermon on the Mount, the

Son of God commands us to pray in private. Later, the desert fathers and mothers—Christian mystics and hermits who fled the cultural, watered-down faith emerging in the fourth century in order to cultivate Christlikeness through contemplative practice in the desert—believed that private prayer was not optional but essential for authentic discipleship. There was a saint at that time called Abba Moses. One day a fellow disciple came to him asking where to find wisdom. Abba Moses echoed Jesus's instruction, saying, "Go and sit in your cell, and your cell will teach you everything."[3] There are things God wants to show us in private that we will not discover in public.

When Jesus instructs us to pray in secret, the word he uses for room is *tameion*. It can also be translated as "pantry" or "closet." In first-century Judea, this word referred to the place where one went to meet with God alone. I suggest this word usage carries at least two meanings:

One is an external geography → the home.
The other is an internal anatomy → the heart.

Let's begin with external geography. In first-century Judea, the common family did not live in a house with many rooms. Most rooms were shared spaces. A robust, private life was a luxury few could afford.[4] When Jesus uses the term *tameion* here, many scholars believe he is referring to a pantry-like room. This room would have been located in the center of a dwelling, without windows. It was here that a family stored dry goods. This context would promote at least two things:

1. Privacy. Devoid of windows, this room decreased the possibility of a person being seen as they prayed.
2. Sincerity. Matthew begins this chapter recording Jesus's caution of hypocrisy. Hypocrisy (Greek: *hypokrites*) is "to

act with a mask on, to be a false self," describing a pretentious person.[5] He rebukes people with a religious spirit
who show off their faith publicly but lack an inner relationship with God. Praying alone in a room reduces the
temptation to pray with improper motives.

Later in chapter 6, Matthew records Jesus using this same term
for room (*tameion*) when referring to the birds: "They do not sow
or reap or store away in barns [*tameion*], and yet your heavenly
Father feeds them" (v. 26). This usage supports the interpretation
of a pantry or storage room in a home being the geographical
location to pray in private.

Gerald Sittser, theologian and author of *Water from a Deep
Well*, states, "Involvement in the world has its place, for God calls
us to serve the world. But we need distance and quiet too, or the
busyness, noise, demands and pressures of the world will consume
us."[6] Finding a pantry where you can regularly meet with God in
private is essential. Consider where this place might be for you. It
could be a room, an office, a chair, a church, or wherever you can
seek God in the silence.

However, there is another dimension to the term that needs
to be explored: internal anatomy. When Jesus taught, he often
spoke on many levels at once. It was a dynamic feature of his teaching ministry and is especially true of his parables. It is plausible
that Jesus was teaching his disciples to enter not only an external
geographical location in the home when they prayed but also an
internal place in their anatomy—namely, the deepest part of themselves. In other words, he was inviting them to delve into the depths
of the soul where the image of God is imprinted and where the
Holy Spirit would dwell after Pentecost. Bruce Demarest calls this
an "inner Sinai,"[7] a sacred meeting space for you and the divine.

The haunting challenge is whether or not we are entering into
our own depths when we go to God in prayer. Perhaps this explains
the chronic boredom in prayer that many claim to experience.

It is far too easy to launch shallow prayers in God's direction on our way out the door. James addresses this in his epistle when he describes the scattered church as those who "do not have because [they] do not ask God" (4:2). And when they do ask, they do not receive because their prayers are in alignment with the flesh and not God's will (v. 3). James is referring to people who avoid the hard work of entering the external and the internal pantry and sitting long enough to discover who they really are and what they really want.

Our prayer lives are often so overly entrenched in hurry, worry, and circumstance that we rarely consider, let alone pray from, the deepest core of who we are. We pray from the top of our minds, and our minds are wrapped up in daily dramas and cyclical monologues. This is not to say that God is disinterested in our dramas. Far from it, actually. But the peace God gives within our circumstances most often comes through connecting with God in our deepest selves and recognizing that many of the dramas we think are urgent are rather fleeting and ultimately meaningless. It is when we move into the depths of the soul that the peace of God can really meet us. It is there that we realize everything is more than okay.

Jesus invites us to seek out an internal monastery within ourselves. Martin Laird said it best: "The only monastery we all need to enter is the one Jesus opened up as he disclosed the inner depths of his own identity and purpose: 'I and the Father are one' (John 10:30)."[8] To obey Jesus's command, we don't have to add another room to our houses, because the room is already fashioned inside our bodies. The inner room is the soul. And Jesus commands us to go there and pray.

The Tabernacle Within

Think of your body—which is the new temple for God's indwelling presence according to 1 Corinthians 6:19—as a wonder

created by God with deeper and deeper rooms within. The Holy
Spirit resides at the core of your being. If you are wrestling with
this biblical analogy, consider the architecture of the tabernacle in
the Hebrew Scriptures. The tabernacle was a tripartite structure,
meaning it contained three distinct spaces (or rooms): the courtyard, the Holy Place, and the Most Holy Place (Exod. 26–27).
Imagine these as levels, each with increasing access to God's holy
presence. Thus, God's presence increases in intensity as one transi-
tions from the courtyard to the Holy Place to the Most Holy Place.
Long after the age of the tabernacle, the New Testament authors
made the staggering claim that Jesus sent the Holy Spirit to dwell
not merely "with us" but "in us." This is why Jesus said to his disciples with clear conviction that it is better that he depart so that
the Holy Spirit could be sent to them (John 16:7). Jesus's ministry
inaugurated a new age of creation in which the Spirit would not
simply dwell with creation but indwell the new creation—namely,
human beings surrendered to Christ as Lord (2 Cor. 1:22; Eph.
1:13; Col. 1:27).

Let's take all that and consider the profundity: human beings—
not the tabernacle, nor the Jerusalem temple—have become the
new location for God's indwelling presence. Just as the tabernacle
in the wilderness was meant to be temporary, the Jerusalem temple
was also meant to be temporary. Both were structures made by
human hands that pointed forward to a better temple—that is,
God's indwelling presence in redeemed human beings, referred to
in Greek as *ekklesia*, and known to us as the church.

Think of the three distinct tabernacle rooms stated above as
your body. The courtyard can be likened to our surface sense of
self. I don't use the term "surface" in a negative way, but more
like Maslow's hierarchy of needs: safety needs (security, physical
health) and psychological needs (food, water, sleep). Think of the
Holy Place within us as our esteem: our need for belonging. Last,
imagine the deepest part of you as the Most Holy Place. This is
the place of deepest identity and belovedness. This is the inner

chamber where God dwells. Consider the possibility that we spend much of our lives spiritually on the surface layers, preoccupied with safety and security prayers (e.g., "God protect me and provide . . ."). Those forms of prayer are well and good, yet the invitation is to go deeper into the inner rooms of our souls, where the Spirit dwells and longs to speak peace to our anxieties, fears, and worries. You were created for depth. God dwells within you and desires for you to go into your inmost room and encounter God's presence there in stillness, silence, and solitude.

A Deeper Path

There is yet another dimension of the spiritual life that we must explore before moving forward. The dominant metanarrative of our time denies the existence of the mystical and metaphysical. Therefore, reality, for the average person today, is limited to what can be observed and proven by a post-Enlightenment scientific way of knowing. Philosopher Charles Taylor has called this the "immanent frame," wherein life is reduced to what we can sense and measure scientifically.[9] But Jesus invites us to explore a deeper reality.

Have you ever noticed the way Jesus refers to his parables? Reminding his disciples of the prophet Isaiah, he says, "I speak to them in parables: 'Though seeing, they do not see; though hearing, they do not hear or understand'" (Matt. 13:13). The Gospels frequently record Jesus instructing his followers to hear and see on two levels. The first is the cognitive level, where we process, sift, and analyze what has been said or encountered. This level often acts as a filter, causing us to either accept or reject a claim. The scientific worldview, which we are taught as early as primary school, is the dominant filter that we in the Western Hemisphere use to evaluate what is and is not possible. This explains why many disbelieve or attempt to explain away the kingdom of God.

The second level is the spiritual level, where we evaluate a claim and, after affirming it as rationally plausible, empower the claim to have a transformative effect on us. Seldom do we get to this level because we are too frightened to examine the false foundations on which our reasoning stands. Furthermore, spiritual learning regularly strikes such a blow to our constructed ego that most are not prepared to receive it. Thus, time and again in Scripture and today, many walk away from Jesus sad or unchanged.

Consider this: Christ invites us to go beyond hearing to really hear—to go beyond seeing to really see. In other words, there are ever-deeper realms into which we are called to commune with God and to gain more understanding. I am not referring to a pseudo-gnostic understanding given only to the elite and privileged few. I am talking about moving beyond superficial spirituality, which is often contaminated with individualism, consumerism, cognition, and safety. When we move beyond superficial spirituality, we enter into a pool whose depths are unfathomable.

This invitation to really hear and see is the invitation of con-templative spirituality. As with two mirrors on opposite walls, the reflection into deeper and deeper images never ceases. This is the spirituality we are invited into. It is not a spirituality that boasts, "I get God" but one that confesses, "God has me." It is not a spirituality that closes the imagination down but one that opens it up. It transforms prayer from talking to God into a practice of being with God. If that appeals to your spirit, let's journey farther.

◆ PRACTICE ◆

The late priest Thomas Keating introduced a term called "centering prayer" to describe the practice that leads one into the inner room of the soul. Here, centering prayer will be utilized as a practice to usher you deeper into prayer.

Find a quiet and comfortable place to sit. Rest both feet on the floor so as not to restrict blood flow. Select a word or phrase that you can connect with your breathing. This should not be a long word or phrase, because you are going to pair it with your inhalation and exhalation. For example, if your phrase is "Come, Lord Jesus," then inhale the word "Come" and exhale "Lord Jesus." This word or phrase is used to keep your mind from wandering.

Set a timer for ten minutes and breathe in and out with your word or phrase, eventually letting yourself rest in silence. If your mind wanders, gently return to your word or phrase. When you realize your mind has wandered, don't be hard on yourself or spend energy analyzing why you lost your way. Simply return to your word and into stillness. After ten minutes, reflect on the experience in your journal.

STILL

Truly my soul finds rest in God;
my salvation comes from him.

—Psalm 62:1

I have discovered that all the unhappiness of men arises from
one single fact, that they are unable to stay quietly in their
own chamber.

—Blaise Pascal, *Pensées*

STILLNESS IS THE FORGOTTEN TEACHER for a society of perpetual movement. Movement means busyness, busyness leads to production, and production yields a bottom line, which in a capitalist society is often our highest ideal. This trajectory is no longer a slice of the pie chart called life; it is the whole pie. Steve Jobs once commented that he was as proud of the things Apple hadn't done as the things Apple had done.[1] In other words, sometimes saying no is as powerful and necessary as saying yes. Further, saying no to the wrong things opens us to opportunities to say yes to the right things. Stillness puts us in touch with greater conviction concerning what to say yes and no to.

But if we are honest, we too often strive for productivity to the neglect of stillness. And so the slogan that defines us is "Don't slow down." We feel the constant urge to produce, and we long for instant gratification. Look no further than the way many of us frequently (or obsessively) check for "likes" to our recent social media posts. Dopamine hits are addictive. And the more we seek them, the more we want them; the more we get them, the more we need them. In this kind of world, it is no wonder that stillness is forgotten. I mean, who has time for that?

Years ago, in morning prayer, I sensed the Holy Spirit whisper a sentence into my heart during the season of Lent:

> Our addiction to immediacy tempts us to settle for accessible substitutes rather than waiting for what we really long for.

I was convicted, to say the least. My brain tends toward efficiency, productivity, and achievement. These tendencies, if not kept in check, can cloud the soul. I imagine the soul as a jar of pure water, and these tendencies as causing the pure water to be saturated with sediment. To gain clarity in life, we need to still our minds and bodies daily in order to let the sediment of our hurried lives slowly sink to the bottom. As an Enneagram Type 3, stillness is no easy task for me. But in that season of Lent, I began to wonder if stillness is not a foe to resist but a gift to embrace. Stillness is the divine invitation to zoom out in order to scan our life horizon and discover what it is we really long for. The prayer poetry of Sister Ruth, the humble Carmelite nun, is deeply instructive here:

> O God, let me climb through the barriers of sound
> And pass into your silence;
> And then, in stillness and silence let me adore You,
> Who are Life-Light-Love
> Without beginning and without end.[2]

A Different Kind of Conference

Have you ever attended a conference that rocked your world? Years back I attended one on the topic of stillness prayer in Santa Fe, New Mexico. Up until then, I assumed the sole point of every conference was for me to cherry-pick ideas, artfully steal concepts, then integrate them into my own vision. But this particular conference was different (perhaps that was what compelled me). The core message rejected the values of increased productivity and idea generation. Instead, each speaker homed in on cultivating divine intimacy through subtracting from life, not adding more; through simplicity, not complexity; through slowing down, not speeding up. It was refreshing—and shocking—from the start.

The room was packed. I hadn't expected that. Thousands were seated in a massive conference room. I guess we were all in search of something similar. Arriving late on the first day, I sat in the last seat available, in the back against the far wall. The keynote speaker, sitting behind a little table at the front, was dwarfed by the size of the room, so his image was projected on giant video screens.

Because I had arrived late, I furtively unzipped my laptop case, opened my computer, created a fresh document, and began typing profusely. With stealth-like ferocity, my fingers captured the wise musings of the speaker and displayed them onto my screen. The guy's speech was on fire! Utterly captivated, I could have heard a pin drop between sentences.

But soon a problem emerged. And I shortly realized the problem was me. Ever been there? Not fun.

As I pecked away at my computer, the woman next to me leaned toward me and not so gently whispered, "Would you mind putting away your computer?"

Put my computer away? How, then, would I capture all these ideas?

Her tone suggested she was making a statement, not asking a question. So as not to make a scene, I obliged. Returning the computer to my bag, I scanned the room. I was one of two people among thousands who had bothered to bring a computer and, as far as I could tell, was one of five not currently drawing a social security check. Why were the attendees so old?

During the lunch hour, I curiously stumbled into conversations with strangers, asking them why they had come to this conference. After half a dozen conversations, I put it all together. Humans eventually come to a place of feeling maxed out and exhausted from decades of production. This is true in the realms of vocation, parenting, and religion. We wonder what it is all supposed to mean. And in dire need of subtracting the minutiae of life, in our latter years, we seek new perspectives to find meaning. The current framework for finding meaning is not wrong, but it overpromises and underdelivers. As Father Richard Rohr espoused in his work *Falling Upward*, we need this construction in the first half of life to awaken us to what we really long for in the second half.[3] Like hoarders, we have filled our brains with decades of information for which we often find no use later in life. In fact, the cognitive overload often weighs us down and crowds out what really matters. Can you relate?

Thousands of people had come to this conference to learn the art of subtraction. They had heard enough sermons, visited enough places, and created impressive résumés only to conclude that contentment and peace are not "out there" waiting to be accessed. St. Augustine said, "Why do you want to speak and not want to listen? You are always rushing out of doors but are unwilling to return into your own house. Your teacher is within."[4] For Christians, the secret of spirituality is that God waits to be discovered within the inner room, and stillness is one of the primary pathways by which a deep level of intimacy with him can be found.

Modes of Spirituality

Western Christianity, particularly the Protestant tradition (of which I am a part), has largely emphasized cataphatic spirituality nearly to the exclusion of apophatic spirituality. Together, they form two sides of the same coin. "Cataphatic" is formed from two words meaning "descend" and "speak." When combined, they create a word that means "to bring God down in such a way so as to speak of God."[5] Cynthia Bourgeault defines cataphatic prayer as "prayer that makes use of what theologians call our 'faculties.' It engages our reason, memory, imagination, feeling, and will. These are the normal human operating systems that connect us with the outer world and to our own interior life. . . . They are wonderful tools. . . . Cataphatic prayer is most of what we are about in church."[6]

This mode of spirituality is satisfied by the fruit of progress. Developing theology, hearing a "word" from God, memorizing Scripture, seeing visions, singing songs, making confession, and accessing clarity are all meaningful activities within cataphatic spirituality.

The other, often neglected, side of the coin is apophatic spirituality. Bourgeault describes it as that which "bypasses our capacities for reason, imagination, visualization, emotion and memory. . . . It, too, makes use of faculties, but ones that are much more subtle than we're used to and which are normally blocked by over-reliance on our more usual mental processing modes."[7]

Whereas the cataphatic is satisfied with doing and knowing, the apophatic is satisfied with being. Both belong, yet we must recover the one that has been lost.

Apophatic spirituality is unappealing to many in a fast-paced, overproductive society because it is unproductive by nature. Dietrich Bonhoeffer provides a helpful defense to this inaccurate assumption: "To be silent does not mean to be inactive; rather it means to breathe in the will of God, to listen attentively and be ready to obey."[8] Jesus did only what he saw the Father doing (John 5:19). How are we to perceive God's present activity if our hearts are busy and not still? Furthermore, perhaps we underestimate God's desire to simply be with us. Maybe God's active presence within us is far more relational than transactional, motivated more by being with us than by producing from us.

When you think about these two modes of spirituality, which side do you have a tendency to overemphasize?

Stillness in the Bible

Jesus knew the importance of intimacy with God and being still in his presence. As we consider a life of contemplative prayer, Jesus offers an example to follow. L. Paul Jensen's work, *Subversive Spirituality*, brilliantly displays moments in the Gospels when Jesus slips away to be with God. Consider the following:

Event	Reference
Temptation	Matthew 4:1–11; Mark 1:11–13; Luke 4:1–13
Early morning prayer	Mark 1:35; Luke 4:42
Pattern of withdrawal	Luke 5:16
Retreating with disciples	Matthew 5–7
Away for rest	Matthew 14:13; Mark 6:30–32; Luke 9:10
Evening prayer	Matthew 14:22–33; Mark 6:45–52
Transfiguration	Matthew 17:1–13; Mark 9:2–13; Luke 9:28–36
Last Supper	Matthew 26:17–30; Mark 14:12–26; Luke 22:14–39
Gethsemane	Matthew 26:36–46; Mark 14:32–42; Luke 22:39–46

Source: L. Paul Jensen, *Subversive Spirituality: Transforming Mission through the Collapse of Space and Time* (Eugene, OR: Pickwick, 2007), 86–87.

One could reasonably conclude that during his wilderness temptation, Jesus did not talk at or with God for forty days straight. In the stillness, he observed what the Father was doing and responded to Satan in the way he did as a result. Jesus knew the value of stilling the soul, away from the crowd, as a way of equipping him to return effectively to the crowd. He valued the inner room before pursuing an outward ministry.

Driving home his point, Jensen legitimizes his case using the example of social media.

Social media is an outlet to live life incessantly directed toward the world. We continuously "check in" to give and receive messages to and from the world. It is perpetual information acquisition. Even when we leave "the world" and return home for the evening, we are still oriented toward the crowd. But Jesus often oriented life away from the crowd. Jesus never "checked in" with the crowd. He only found himself in the crowd after being empowered from solitude.[9]

We find this kind of spirituality in the Hebrew Scriptures (Old Testament) as well. Many of the Psalms are an expression of soul desperation. They were not often written by those touting inner tranquility by the seaside. David penned many of them in the midst of profound anxiety, fear, and relational conflict. Many of them were written on the run. Many of them were penned when the world was splitting at the seams.

In Psalm 62, David is up to his eyeballs—as they say—in conflict and despair. It's in that place, in the midst of chaos, unrest, and stress, that David seeks not to be reactive but to actively seek God in stillness, trusting that God is at work.

> Truly my soul finds rest in God;
>   my salvation comes from him. . . .
> Truly he is my rock and my salvation;
>   he is my fortress, I will not be shaken. (vv. 1, 6)

David is fleeing for his life. Pressed against the wall, he faces opponents on every side. Ever been there? David's spirituality models for us that clarity and peace are not to be discovered within the crowds (praising us) or the chaos (upending us). Rather, they are found in hollowing out a still place to be with the living God. Have you created such a place in your life?

Cultivating Stillness

Martin Laird contends that pursuing habits of stillness in life is not in opposition to an active life but rather to a reactive life.[10] So many of our current patterns of behavior center on responding to life's persistent intrusions and notifications. Removing the cell phone from one's reach is, for some, an exercise requiring great discipline. We have become accustomed to continuous reaction and thus have forfeited a life of genuine conviction, authenticity, and action.

Stillness is a great teacher. In a society of activity, we must again take it seriously if we are to fully return to who God says we are. The fruits of cultivating stillness are a greater awareness of God and self and an increased clarity about life.

The Greek mystic Diadochus likens the mind to the sea: "When the sea is calm, fishermen can scan its depths and therefore hardly any creature moving in the water escapes their notice. But when the sea is disturbed by the winds it hides beneath its turbid and agitated waves what it was happy to reveal when it was smiling and calm; and then the fishermen's skill and cunning prove vain. The same thing happens with the contemplative power of the intellect."[11]

The problem isn't that the waters are merely murky. The problem is that they are raging. Once we diagnose that reality, stillness permits us to quiet them. And as we quiet the tides of the mind, we can begin to see clearly to the bottom, recognizing who we are and what we are after. According to Laird, when we still ourselves, "the ocean depth of awareness can be gazed into. This is the invitation of interior silence. We look right into the mind, right into awareness itself in which thoughts and feelings appear and disappear, whether they are like troubled, stormy waters or feathery ocean foam."[12]

There is a reason that being still with God is an often-omitted practice: stillness is hard and requires discipline. But this pathway of discipline is not only biblical but also historic. Henri Nouwen defined this discipline as "the effort to create some space in which God can act."[13] Evagrius of Ponticus believed that "the practice of stillness is full of joy and beauty."[14] Truly, it is in stillness that we calm the sea of the soul long enough to become aware of what we really need.

◆ PRACTICE ◆

In his simple book of prayer, Pete Greig writes, "To start we must stop. To move forward we must pause. This is the first step in a deeper prayer life: Put down your wish list and wait. Sit quietly. 'Be still, and know that I am God.'"[15] Return again to the practice of centering prayer. This time, set the timer for twelve minutes. Afterward, record observations about the experience in your journal.

GROANS

In the same way, the Spirit helps us in our weakness. We do not know what we ought to pray for, but the Spirit himself intercedes for us through wordless groans. And he who searches our hearts knows the mind of the Spirit, because the Spirit intercedes for God's people in accordance with the will of God.

—Romans 8:26–27

Have you considered what an astonishing promise it is that the Spirit prays in us, and does so "according to the will of God"?

—Marjorie J. Thompson, *Soul Feast*

PAUL WRITES that "we do not know what we ought to pray for" (Rom. 8:26). "We" is that part of us we most often identify as the "surface" self, if you will. Although that part of us is a piece of who we are, it is not our deepest, truest identity. Therefore, when we identify most with this part of ourselves, we do not pray from the deeper room within.

In 2007, I moved from pastoring a large community in central
Florida to planting a church in Southern California. Everything
about church planting that one needs to know, but soon forgets,
is implied in the term itself: the vocation requires the patience of
a farmer rather than the efficiency of a machinist. Self-imposed
deadlines, relentless fundraising, and chronic comparison tragically turn church *planters* into church *mechanics*. Several months
into the project, I was exhausted at every level. I needed a breakthrough, but I wasn't sure what kind of breakthrough I needed.

Around that time, a friend was hosting a workshop in East
Hollywood (of all places) that centered on the life and ministry of
Henri Nouwen. Nouwen had left a prestigious faculty position at
Yale to serve and live alongside people with cognitive disabilities in
a community outside Toronto called Daybreak. Nouwen's life had
been characterized by the same struggles we all face: comparison,
control, and consumption. Those three Cs were the merry-go-
round in my head; perhaps they are in yours too.

At a break in the workshop, another attendee and I struck up
a conversation that turned into a long discussion over lunch. We
were commiserating about the pressures of life and our yearning
to connect more deeply with God. I sometimes find it sobering to reconcile the depth of our spiritual ancestors' faith with
the superficiality we see in much of Western Christianity. The
more we talked, the more I realized this man had developed the
disciplines necessary to move beyond *talking at God* to *being
with God*. I sensed God had sent me this man to help me name
the breakthrough I was waiting for. By the end of lunch, I could
articulate what I had previously intuited but had been unable
to name. I wanted a deeper relationship with God (think Mary
at the feet of Jesus, not Martha doing chores around the house)
that was in line with those of the early church, the desert fathers
and mothers, the monastic communities, and many other Christian traditions.

It occurred to me that maybe it was time to stop riding the merry-go-round in my mind, that maybe there was a better conversation I needed to join. And maybe that conversation wasn't taking place "out there" but was already present within me through the Holy Spirit. This is where Romans 8:26–27 came into play. Marjorie J. Thompson, a Presbyterian spiritual director, says it well: "Have you considered what an astonishing promise it is that the Spirit prays in us, and does so 'according to the will of God'? Perhaps our real task in prayer is to attune ourselves to the conversation already going on deep in our hearts. Then we may align our conscious intentions with the desire of God being expressed at our core."[1]

In Romans 8, Paul rightly confesses that we do, in fact, have weaknesses. Further, the Spirit within us longs to help us where we are weak. The problem is that the three Cs of comparison, control, and consumption are subversive strategies we employ to strive in our own capacities. The neural pathways in our brains have dug entrenched tracks over a lifetime that reinforce the three Cs. They are our muscle memory. (We will talk about the neurology of spiritual formation later.) We equate strength with feeling equipped and competent in our abilities. We believe the illusion that comparing ourselves to others can lead to personal victory. We swallow whole the lie that if we can only control our lives through worry, manipulation, and striving, then we will achieve what we are hoping for. We are seduced into thinking that being fully alive means consuming the next product, latest gadget, or newest experience. Perhaps these are the very weaknesses from which the Holy Spirit—who lives within us—seeks to liberate us.

In this text, Paul is implying that we are so caught up in our inner dramas that we lack the clarity to know what to pray for. We are so lost in our heads that we don't even know it, so lost that we assume we are found. Jesus told the Pharisees that their problem wasn't their blindness but their belief that they could see (John 9:41). That's not just lost, but *lost* lost.

Finding our way back requires us to pursue the inverse of our natural impulses:

stillness

silence

surrender

Surrendering to the indwelling Holy Spirit connects us to the eternal dialogue happening within the Trinity. This conversation that the Trinity has been having since creation is a far better conversation than the one happening in our heads. And entering this better conversation reminds us of what is true. The truth is twofold:

1. We are probably less important than we think.
2. We are definitely more loved than we know.

When we first discover that we are less important than we think, the discovery can create a loss of significance. But this is a grace to us. It's a grace because our self-worth no longer has to be forged and defended through comparison, control, and consumption. What liberation! When we get to that place, we then can fully embrace the reality that we are more loved than we know. This is why Christians claim wholeheartedly that identity is received, not achieved. God's great love for us brings us, in Christ through the Holy Spirit, into the current of the Triune God. All we must do is surrender to it.

So maybe we should get off the donkey going around the mill and enter the eternal conversation, where we can discover the joy and the mystery of what the Holy Spirit is constantly speaking with the Father and the Son. This conversation within the Trinity is full of sacrifice, acceptance, and creative love toward the other. Isn't this a better conversation than the inner chatter of critique and ego?

The Groaning of the Spirit

Paul says that the Holy Spirit is groaning inside us (Rom. 8:26–27). In the Bible, the Greek word for "groaning" is *stenagmois*. But what does that mean? Paul claims that the Holy Spirit lives within us and offers mysterious utterance to the Father and the Son within the depths of who we are. That sounds kind of weird, doesn't it? But these groanings are intercessions on our behalf. So when I say that we should join a better conversation, this is the conversation I am referring to. The essential task in prayer may not be to *start* a new conversation with God but rather to join the eternal conversation already happening within us. The Triune God is already having a conversation within us, through the Holy Spirit. The contemplative life is about learning to join that conversation. Prayer doesn't begin with us talking and end when we run out of things to say. Prayer is always happening between the Father, the Son, and the Holy Spirit. And the Holy Spirit, who lives in the center of our being, always invites us to pull up a chair and join.

Scholars have explored what this mysterious utterance (*stenagmois*) of the Spirit might be like. New Testament professor Douglas Moo insists that the groans of the Spirit are "'unspoken,' never rising to the audible level at all."[2] Moo says that "our failure to know God's will and our consequent inability to petition God specifically and assuredly is met by God's Spirit, who Himself expresses to God those intercessory petitions that perfectly match the will of God."[3]

Paul's instruction in Romans 8 is perhaps the strongest admonition in the epistles to quiet the mind and attune the soul to silence, for it is only in the silence that we hear God's whispers of liberation that release us from the burden of establishing and defending our own significance. People sometimes ask me what to believe about God when we experience God's silence. This is a fair question and deserves pondering. It has been said that God's first language is silence, because, through Christ's sacrifice of love on the cross, God no longer has anything to say against us. What if God's silence is, therefore, not an absence but instead an affirmation of our acceptance? What if God's silence simply indicates that God no longer has anything to say against us because of the blood of Jesus? Something to ponder, indeed.

Surrendering to the Spirit

One of the criticisms of contemplative prayer is that it is surrendering into nothingness. Many skeptics have compared contemplation to diving into a pool that may or may not have water to support us. But unlike Buddhist meditation, which is a dive into an opaque vastness with the goal of transcending desire, Christian contemplation is a dive into the Holy Spirit. Rather than falling into nothing, we fall into Someone. And the Holy Spirit never calls us to flee all desire. The problem isn't with desire but with disordered desire. Through contemplative prayer, we realign our desires with God's desires. We do not need to fear surrendering to God in silence and stillness, for it is the Spirit of Christ who awaits our company and invites us into the conversation.

When I first began praying this way, both my thoughts and my body fought my efforts to be still. Not only was my mind racing, but my body was suddenly alive with pangs and impulses that distracted me. I discovered that sitting up in a comfortable position with both feet on the floor so as not to constrict blood flow helped calm my body, but I often wondered what to do with the chatter in my head.

The desert fathers and mothers taught that the outward posture of prayer helps form the inward reality. When moving into still and silent prayer, it is helpful to bend one's head toward the heart. This position reflects the priority of the heart informing the mind rather than the other way around. Again, there is nothing wrong with the mind, but for many of us, the mind has always been the seat of control over all our other faculties. This posture serves to balance our approach in prayer. Not only is bending the head toward the heart a restful position, but it also serves as a reminder that in contemplation the heart is steering the ship. Martin Laird clarifies what the heart is and how we encounter the risen Christ there: "The heart, a term that refers not to our thoughts and feelings but to our innermost depths that ground thought and feeling, our knowing center, is the place of divine encounter. Just because the Risen Christ is not accessible to the senses in the way the historical Jesus was, this does not imply absence but draws us to a Presence that is deeper than our discursive and imagining powers can perceive, but in which the heart delights."[4]

This reminds me time and again that my mind must submit to the Spirit, who lives within the center of my being. For me, this is a posture of submission to the voice of the Spirit. This is the posture in which I can begin to hear the groans of the Spirit within me intercede according to the will of God. Perhaps such a posture will help you do the same.

♦ PRACTICE ♦

The Eastern Orthodox Church has long practiced the tradition of praying a few short lines known as the Jesus Prayer. The Jesus Prayer focuses on repeating a simple refrain:

Inhale: *Lord Jesus Christ*
Exhale: *Have mercy on me*

This condensed form of the Jesus Prayer centers our identity on the person of Christ. It acknowledges our inadequacy as sinners apart from the mercy of God, and it gives the mind something to focus on as we open ourselves up to the groaning of the Holy Spirit.

Set a timer for five to fifteen minutes today and practice this form of prayer. Afterward, record the experience in your journal. Stick to this practice daily for a week and see what opens up for you over time.

DIVE

By waiting and by calm you shall be saved,
in quiet and in trust shall be your strength.
—Isaiah 30:15 (NABRE)

Our meditation must be directed toward God; otherwise
we may spend our time . . . in quiet convers(ation) with ourselves. This may quiet our nerves but will not further our
spiritual life in any way.

—A. W. Tozer, *The Pursuit of God*

I'LL LET YOU in on a secret you probably already know: most
people do not think they are good at prayer. Perhaps we imagine
that everyone else is better at it than we are. Or perhaps we think
we are awesome at prayer, in which case we're probably not very
far down the path of discipleship, because humility is the fruit of
a mature prayer life. Prayer is difficult. We are like embodied fidget
spinners, anxious about life, addicted to productivity, struggling to
be still. More often than not, growing in maturity requires that we
go down an unpleasant path. St. John of the Cross wrote a great
deal about the path of the soul's dark night, which is not exactly
pleasant but nevertheless purposeful. Likewise, the contemplative

prayer life is hard, but the payoff is worth it. As Martin Laird wrote, "Prayer matures by a process of breaking down rather than by acquisition and spiritual prowess."[1]

The twentieth-century Christian mystic Evelyn Underhill believed that the first fifteen minutes of stillness prayer are a time of warfare and struggle.[2] The soul is like an onion that needs to be peeled back, layer by layer. Getting beneath a surface spirituality is a process that takes time and intention. So every time we sit in stillness before the Lord, we must work our way through the veneer in order to descend into the depths. And to be honest, in a culture of rush and hurry, few people seek to do this. Instead, they settle for a superficial spirituality. I don't use that term as a put-down to describe some cheap form of cosmetic Christianity. I use that term in the sense that there is so much more depth for us to plumb. Unfortunately, most churches in America do not lead their people into the deeper paths of being with God.

Because our cultural conditioning demands more words, objectives, and entertainment, it is often difficult for us to maintain focus in contemplative prayer. Therefore, it is helpful when beginning this difficult method of prayer to secure an image in your mind to usher you into prayer and keep you there. To be sure, this is not an image you worship but an image you allow yourself to focus on. You can return to this image (just as you did with a word or phrase in an earlier practice) when your mind drifts. Once you move beyond the entry level of contemplative prayer, you may let go of the image, as it will have served its purpose.

Through my own growth in contemplative prayer, two images have served me well. If the images below are helpful for you, use them. If not, try to come up with an image of your own.

Image One—Flowing River

When I began engaging in contemplative prayer, the first image that helped me was a river gently flowing downstream. When you go to pray, sit in a comfortable position. Breathe deeply in and out. Then close your eyes and imagine yourself on a raft, slowly drifting downstream.

All the conditions are perfect. There is nothing to resist. As you drift downstream, you notice much that entices along the banks. These are good things: friends you know, trees providing shade and rest, towns and cities that beckon you to dock and experience them. You can get off the river and experience any or all of these things, but if you do, you will forfeit what lies at the end of the river: the presence of God. Although the people and places along the banks invite you into good things, were you to disembark and partake, you would forfeit what is better.

The good things along the way represent the good things we might experience if were we not praying, such as new ideas, daily tasks, weekend activities, and so on. Again, these are good things. They just aren't as good as the hallowed moment of our prayer time.

The temptations that seek to pull us off the river and onto the shore are many. It is a daily struggle for me to stay on the raft and drift toward the presence of Jesus rather than disembark and follow all the enticements that come into my mind. For example, I know that if my phone is within arm's reach I will be tempted to pick it up while I'm praying. I am very creative in coming up with all sorts of excuses to justify why I must pick up my phone. You too? Even though I know it is not evil to check my phone, I realize how quickly I can detach from contemplative prayer and attend to other things if I am not careful. Remember, the aim of contemplative prayer is: being, not doing; receiving, not achieving; surrendering, not performing.

Image Two—Deep-Sea Diver

A second image has proven even more helpful to me than the first. It is the image of a deep-sea diver. I begin prayer imagining this scene. I'm a diver whose diving weights are pulling me down to the seafloor. Upon reaching the bottom, I rest in stillness on the floor. It is dark, spacious, and vacuous, similar to how Teresa of Avila described the soul: "The soul is vast, spacious, plentiful."[3] When I look up, I can see the water's surface. Boats skim the surface. These boats represent the chatter in my mind. I desperately want to ascend and explore what the boats contain. I'm intrigued by where the boats are going, and I'm somewhat anxious that I may be missing out as I sit here on the seafloor. I soon discover that I have unintentionally chased the chatter in my mind, and I imagine I've instantaneously returned to the water's surface and am peering over the side of a boat.

This happens often in contemplative prayer. None of us are very good at praying in this way. Just when we think we are being with God, we go chasing ideas in our minds. When this occurs, don't be self-critical, because that just contributes to the noise in your head. Instead, visualize yourself releasing your grip on the boat and surrendering to the gentle weight of God's grace as it takes you back to the water's depths.

In the depths of the sea, there is nothing to produce, attain, or see. You are there simply to be with God in stillness, silence, and solitude. It is good and enough to be in this moment with God. This is what I call "the dive." This image supports contemplation as a state of being, not doing or achieving; surrendering, not performing.

Like strong headwinds are the distractions tempting us to return to the water's surface, especially at first. My own experience aligns with what Laird said so well: "The practice of contemplation can strike us as frustratingly awkward, and we react to everything within and without."[4] So when—not *if*—we find ourselves distracted in prayer, caught up in the chatter of the mind, simply notice it and return to the prayer practice.

We must give ourselves grace when we find that we have surfaced again. God is well aware of (and patient with) our distracted minds. And the grace we give ourselves is mirrored by the grace God is already offering us. So instead of being frustrated when you sense you are not praying well, simply descend again into the water's depths. There you will find God graciously waiting, even when you do not sense it.

Many in the contemplative tradition have described the experience of a scattered prayer life as "monkey mind." Like monkeys in a tree, our thoughts jump from branch to branch. Daniel Goleman asserts, "The inner tug to drift away from effortful focus is so strong that cognitive scientists see a wandering mind as the brain's 'default' mode."[5] The twentieth-century Serbian monk Elder Thaddeus of Vitovnica believed that "the mind is a great wanderer. It is always traveling. It cannot rest until the only One who can lay it to rest appears. . . . And so, this means that our mind cannot attain peace unless the Mighty One, the Holy Spirit, enlightens us. That is when our minds learn to contemplate in the right way, and we come to the realization that quiet and gentle thoughts, full of love and forgiveness, are the way to peace and stillness."[6]

Diving into the depths of God's ocean is one of the most difficult modes of prayer. We are programmed to produce, and sitting with God doesn't usually feel very productive, particularly when we first begin contemplative prayer. However, this practice imparts immense joy over time as we discover that God is not after our production. To be sure, life in Christ does bear fruit, but only after proper watering and exposure to the light bring it into season.

◆ PRACTICE ◆

Set a timer for eighteen minutes. Imagine yourself as a diver in the sea. Now descend to the depths, connect your breath with a word or phrase, and practice contemplative prayer using these four Rs:

1. Resist no thought: don't try too hard not to think, because that will cause you to think.

2. Retain no thought: let thoughts go like an object that floats into a net and then escapes through its holes.

3. React to no thought: don't get caught up in reacting to your thoughts; let them go.

4. Return to your word or phrase.

GAZE

We all, who with unveiled faces contemplate the Lord's glory,
are being transformed into his image with ever-increasing
glory, which comes from the Lord, who is the Spirit.

—2 Corinthians 3:18

You shall gaze upon many things beyond telling, and you
shall hear extraordinarily more things, which you cannot
express with your tongue.

—Saint Symeon, the New Theologian

I MET MY WIFE, ELAINA, at a coffee shop near UCLA.
A mutual friend connected us because Elaina was in search of
a church, and I—having just started a church—was in search of
church members. Everybody wins. Within five minutes of conversation, I was mesmerized. I excused myself to the restroom, where
I called my sister: "Rebecca, I just met my wife." My sister replied,
"AJ, is this actually you on the line?" In an instant, I'd become a
total victim of Cupid. Suffice it to say, we quickly fell in love and

the rest is history. Sadly, that coffee shop is no longer in existence, but our love remains.

Our romantic relationships and our relationship with God share themes. In fact, our relationships with other humans often provide insight into our relationship with the divine. In the initial stages of my budding relationship with Elaina, we talked, and talked, and talked. We stayed up into the wee hours of the night steeped in conversation around topics both shallow and deep, and everywhere in between. Due to absurd traffic in LA, I would wait until late in the night to drive home to Long Beach from her house in Santa Monica. If you've ever driven I-405 (the 405, as it's called), then you know what I'm talking about.

Remember those first stages of romance? The heart palpitates, the palms sweat, and you sacrifice sleep just to talk into the night. Exploring someone's life, discovering another's longings, and discerning your level of commitment to the relationship are done largely through verbal communication in these initial stages. This is perhaps what scares many about a lifelong marriage commitment:

"What if we run out of things to say to each other?"
"I like this person now, but what if I'm not interested in this person in ten, twenty, or fifty years?"

It's taken me more than a decade of marriage to answer these questions, and here is what I've discovered:

1. Words are the beginning of relational intimacy, but not the summit.
2. Human beings are dynamic and not static.

We are always changing; we are always growing in one direction or another. We know this to be true on a cellular level. Did you know that around one million cells in your body die every second and then are replaced by brand-new ones? If change is a constant on a cellular level, it stands to reason that change is a constant on a relational and spiritual level too.

The Greek philosopher Heraclitus is said to have uttered, "You can never step into the same river twice." People, too, like a river, undergo continuous change. The only way you can wake up disinterested in your spouse fifty years from now is if you stop being curious about who they are becoming today. Many of those who have committed to another person for the long haul of life will tell you that the deepest level of relational intimacy transpires after we run out of words to say. An entry level of intimacy needs words. But at a deeper level of intimacy, we can look into each other's eyes and connect beyond words.

Relationally (and spiritually) I refer to this as "the gaze." What is true for us horizontally (with humans) is also true for us vertically (with God). This is where contemplative prayer comes in. We can just be with God. It bears repeating: we need words in our relationships with God and one another. With God, words help us intercede, give thanks, confess, praise, and so forth. However, consider this: maybe our conversations with God have only just begun when we're out of words to say. For too long, I assumed that my conversations with God were over when I was done talking. Paraphrasing the lament of Sandra Bullock's character in *Gravity*, no one taught me otherwise.

The Intimacy of Silence

Pause for a moment and let this core truth sink in: God is eternally available. For someone as self-preoccupied as I am, it is a marvel that whenever I want to stop thinking about myself and seek to connect with God, I am met with divine communion. No matter the scenario—in the car, on a walk, at dinner—God is always available and desirous to commune with his creation. The Greek and Roman gods pale in comparison to the goodness of the Trinity.

To answer Philip Yancey's great question, this is what is so amazing about grace. Every moment of every day, the most significant happening in the entire universe is the radical availability of God's presence. Yet in almost every moment of every day, we remain unaware of this generous gift.

These past few years I have discovered the intimacy of silence. This silence is not a void but a place inhabited by a Presence—a Presence that is infinite and, because of Christ's work, desires to dwell within us without words or accusation. In the silence, we meet God's gaze. It is there that we experience forgiveness, acceptance, and the joy of being fully known.

From a human-to-human perspective, this is the beautiful moment when we sit across the table from someone and can simply be together. This wordless way of being together represents a depth of intimacy rather than a lack. Words are welcomed but not essential. Our relationship with God is no different.

For many reasons, most people avoid relating to the divine in this way. Marjorie Thompson recounts a story of an eighteenth-century priest who asked an old peasant what he did all those hours spent sitting in the chapel. The peasant said, "I look at Him, He looks at me, and we are happy."[1] This is spirituality at its zenith. What we discover when we gaze at the Lord in silent prayer is that he is gazing back at us. New Testament scholar Kenneth Bailey writes that the ancient rabbis would arrive to morning prayer one hour early just to stand (not sit) in silence in order to prepare their hearts to commune with God.[2] Silence before God both prepares and transforms us.

Italian Catholic writer Carlo Carretto claimed, "True prayer demands that we be more passive than active; it requires more silence than words, more adoration than study, more concentration than rushing about, more faith than reason."[3] But I will warn you again: being with God is difficult. We aren't conditioned for it. So when you sense yourself failing while praying, perhaps these words from Francis de Sales will encourage you: "If the heart wanders or is distracted . . . bring it back to the point quite gently . . . though it went away every time, your hour would be very well-employed."[4]

Mary, the mother of Jesus, is the premier example of this posture. When greeted by the angel, she pondered and treasured the mystery in her heart. She recognized that God's gift of presence, love, and favor had come upon her through grace. She did not earn the gift by religious activity, for if she had, it would no longer be a gift. In her posture of consent and surrender, she humbly received God's plan for her life and treasured the relationship that was growing within her.

Do you realize this Presence lives inside you? If you are in Christ, the divine Presence that Mary housed in her womb for nine long months is the same Presence that dwells inside you through the Holy Spirit. Jesus, according to John, affirmed, "We [meaning the Trinity] will come to them and make our home with them" (John 14:23). God is closer than our breath, and we are invited to be with God beyond talking at or with God. We are invited into a gaze.

In the gaze with God, we are invited to become less active and more passive.

In the gaze with God, we can use less words and more silence.

In the gaze with God, we are summoned to less information and more adoration.

In the gaze with God, we can rest in less reason and more surrender.

Blank Space

In Japanese art, there is a concept called "ma." Ma refers to empty, blank space on a canvas. Rather than perceiving that blank space as meaningless, needing to be filled, an artist sees it as essential to the piece. The empty space intentionally draws the viewer in and goes to work on the one who gazes. I think God wants to call us into more and more empty space within a busy and broken world. When we are drawn into God's depths, we can begin to understand the way he notices us and apprehend the peace and joy he imparts.

Truly, as we grow in prayer, which is to say, as we grow in our relationship with God, prayer becomes less something we do and more a way of being with God, of being drawn into the life of God.[5] Sound theology helps us to form categories for our relationship with God, but sound theology is not our relationship with God. Mission is the fruit of our relationship with God, but mission is not our relationship with God. Therefore, the praying life is not one of many functions in our relationship with God—it *is* our relationship with God. For many, this is a challenging idea. We much prefer measuring our relationship with God using church commitments, active missionary projects, or theological knowledge. The reason for this preference is because these endeavors tap into the temptation to justify ourselves via ego performance. And performance takes pride in achievement and productivity. I am not opposed to fruit-bearing in the world; God wants us to bear spiritual fruit. But when fruit-bearing is the essence of our spirituality and not the effect, we put the cart in front of the horse. In the end, we are far more comfortable with striving. But striving is not where abundance is found. Striving is the sure pathway to spiritual burnout and exhaustion. God longs for us to serve *from* love, not *for* love. Christian contemplation is the pathway to spiritual maturity and lasting fruit.

This way of prayer—the gaze—is difficult to learn, no doubt. However, once we push through the initial "boredom" and beyond the introductory phases of stillness, prayer as word-filled chatter becomes dissatisfying. We discover that what we previously settled for in prayer no longer brings a fulfilling level of intimacy. The reason for this is that we were created to swim in the depths with God, not splash about in the shallows. In the silence, in the blank space, we meet grace not in a doctrine but in the person of Jesus. As Laird says, "The senses must learn to abide in stillness."[6] And even though you might sense God's silence, do not confuse that with God's absence. It is in the silence we learn to "live by faith, not by sight" (2 Cor. 5:7).

Theologian Hans Urs von Balthasar claimed that "the longer one gazes into this mystery, the more one longs to go on gazing, glimpsing the fulfillment of that to which our entire creaturely nature aspires."[7] Gazing into God becomes the longing we sensed but could never articulate. And the reason we could not articulate it is precisely because words are inadequate to describe the kind of depth God longs for us to experience. The mystery of his infinite nature is enough to occupy our curiosity for a lifetime until we see him face-to-face.

From Solitude to Community to Ministry

An often-employed but misguided critique of contemplative prayer is ostensibly its private nature. The same critique is often doled out to monks, who are misperceived as people seeking to escape society while seeking solitude. However, this is far from being true. Monks generally retreat to the outskirts of the city in order to gain emotional and spiritual "altitude" to properly intercede for it. Further, monks are steeped in community as a way of life. Similarly, the contemplative method of prayer is designed to bring security, freedom, and capacity for the Christian to engage the world.

Henri Nouwen wrote about the trajectory of Jesus's ministry as always moving from solitude to community to ministry.[8] The same is true for those who practice contemplative prayer. The day begins in our inner room, both crying out to and gazing upon God. The resource of prayer is designed to lead us to see others and to respond in light of the kingdom of God. The intimacy with God we experience inwardly through contemplation manifests itself outwardly through action, and this action reflects the work that is being done in us while we gaze upon our God. We must be careful not to wield contemplation for production purposes. But it is clear from the ministry of Jesus that this kind of inward intimacy with the Father produces fruit. We don't have to focus on the results, but the seed scattered in the soil of our praying souls will supernaturally birth love toward our neighbor.

As we awaken to greater self-awareness, we also awaken to an awareness of others' needs. Instead of being engulfed in the noise and distractions of modern life, we receive through contemplation the resources to see and hear ourselves and others. As we embrace the image of God within ourselves (which is always graced and never earned), we see that God has graced everyone with this same image, even those who have yet to receive the Spirit through the confession of Christ as Lord. And we glorify God as we honor God's image in everyone we encounter. As British journalist Oliver Burkeman said, "What will your life have been, in the end, but the sum total of everything you spent it focusing on."[9]

May you experience God within. May you learn the way of being with God. And as you experience more and more of God's eternal availability, may you become the blessing this world is waiting for.

◆ PRACTICE ◆

My friend Ross runs a tool-and-die company in west Michigan. Over a cup of coffee one morning, he leaned in and whispered something I've not forgotten: "I notice each morning in my meditation that I seldom hear anything, yet my soul is always in a different place when I'm finished." As you pray in the silence, don't be discouraged by the silence. Be encouraged that God is at work in deeper ways than words can communicate.

As you become more comfortable with contemplative prayer, set a timer for twenty minutes. Most contemplatives recommend twenty minutes as the minimum time needed to truly enter into the depths of the self and discover God. After twenty minutes, we finally experience release from all the noise and can rest with God. Begin breathing in and out with a word or phrase and sit for twenty minutes. Record the experience in your journal.

PART 3

NEUROLOGY

"CAN I GET A VOLUNTEER?"

A hush fell over the room, then a surge of hands went into the air. I mean, who wouldn't want to have sensors placed on their head so that an audience can see images of their brain while they pray? Everyone in the house was captivated.

At the time, I was the pastor of Mars Hill Bible Church in Grand Rapids, Michigan. While leading an evening contemplative healing service, I invited a fellow church member and neuropsychologist, Timothy Royer ("Doc" from here forward since that is what he prefers to be called), to join me on stage.[1] Over many years of practice, Doc has read over fifty thousand brain scans. So the guy knows his stuff. I had guided the community through the basics of contemplative prayer and invited Doc to lead us from there. He asked if anyone wanted to have sensors put on their head so we could see what happens in the brain when someone prays. Hands surged, and one volunteer was chosen. The place was electric. And it was incredible to see revealed on the screen the brain scan of the volunteer while praying.

Tragically, many wonder, "Is it possible to love science and also believe in God?" As Christians, our response must be, "How can you love science and *not* believe in God?" I believe all good science ends in doxology—*praise God to whom all blessings flow*. Science helps us peer into the mystery. Science offers the *what* and the *how*. Faith helps us with a different set of questions. Faith offers the *why* and the *who*. These disciplines are not in opposition. Faith and science belong together.

People often wonder if anything happens when we pray. They ask questions like "Does prayer work?" "Is prayer effective?" and "Does prayer really change anything?" We can now definitely answer, "Yes! Just look at the screen." One of the ways we peer into brain activity is through an electroencephalogram (EEG). This measures electrical impulses as brain cells communicate with one another. The EEG produces wavy lines on a screen. Praying changes those waves as various brain regions activate and deactivate.

Sufjan Stevens has long had my respect as a music artist. When he first hit the stage, his style was nothing short of fresh, dynamic, and unique. He could effortlessly arrange emotion-laced music with deep lyrical content. He encapsulated the mood of an early 2000s hipster . . . which, of course, I was.

A subtle lyric from his song "Casimir Pulaski Day" on the album *Illinois* haunted me for years. Stevens bravely sang about the challenge of faith in a world filled with tragedy such as cancer. Subtly weaving creative lyrics, he laments that, although they gather to pray for healing at the Tuesday night Bible study, "nothing ever happens."

Now, perhaps what Stevens specifically wanted to happen didn't happen, but medical studies reveal that it is technically (and scientifically) false to say, "Nothing ever happens."

No one is sure what exactly happens when we pray, but if we look at an EEG of someone who is praying, we can say, with conviction, that something happens. Something happens in many places, in fact—the heart and the lungs as well. And what happens doesn't stop with the "hardware" of our bodies. Over time, our "software," such as our character, transforms, and virtues (such as gentleness, kindness, and even self-control) are cultivated. Contemplative prayer can also significantly increase our levels of empathy and patience and our ability to return to peace and joy in the midst of suffering and hardship. Who doesn't want more of that? I do! Truly, we are fearfully and wonderfully made. In the conclusion, I write more specifically about the benefits of contemplative prayer.

What Is the Brain Anyway?

Before diving deep into the chapters in this section, I want to provide some brain basics to ensure we are on the same page. Neuroscientist Andrew Newberg defines the brain as "the conglomeration of neurons and support cells that exists within the human head. This also includes all of the neurotransmitters, chemicals, and blood vessels that make up and allow the brain to function. The 'mind' [is] the thoughts, feelings, and experiences that a given individual may have."[2]

Your brain weighs approximately 3.5 pounds and consumes 20 percent of your daily energy. From a ratio standpoint, that's a large percentage. The oxygen from our lungs helps generate the electrical current that provides our body systems with the energy necessary for life.

Most experts estimate that the average human brain contains somewhere between 80 and 100 billion neurons. These neurons connect to one another through a tiny space called a synaptic cleft. If you do the math, that means there are over 100 trillion neurological connection possibilities. That's a lot. And the more times that two neurons make the same connection, the stronger that connection becomes. The fewer times they make certain connections, the weaker those connections remain. Think of it like tires grinding into mud. The more repetition, the deeper the tracks.

Let's think about the brain in terms of capacity. Benedict Carey writes that "connected [neurons] form a universe of intertwining networks that communicate in a ceaseless, silent electrical storm with a storage capacity, in digital terms, of a million gigabytes."[3] Put another way, we have the brain capacity for up to about three million television shows, give or take. Which means that you could potentially store all 32+ seasons of *The Simpsons* in your head—and then some. The brain stores information like filing cabinets. Not only is there a vast storehouse for data, but information gets sorted in various pathways in the brain.

The brain's function isn't confined to the skull. You've probably heard the phrase "a head on a stick" used to refer to someone who's a genius. Well, no one is a "head on a stick." The brain controls all the nerves distributed throughout the body. For example:

When you move your arm: brain.

When you close your eyes: brain.

When you ride your bike: brain.

When you digest your lunch: brain.

When your gut feels queasy on a first date: brain.

When you're anxious about the future: brain.

When you get a sensation in worship: brain.

When you pray: brain.

We are not a brain and then a body. We are holistic beings, integrated at every level. To love God with all our minds is to seek integration of every system of our being.

Some people today will argue—vehemently, I might add—that change is not possible, that who we are is hardwired from birth or due to social forces outside our control. Christian belief is that change is possible. Paul writes in Romans 12:2 that transformation can happen through the renewing of the mind. In other words, pay attention to what you focus on, strengthen new neural pathways, and new ways of being will open up for you. This certainly isn't the only way transformation happens, but it is definitely one way that it does. The mind is renewed by cooperating in obedience with the Spirit to develop neural pathways that seek what is good, true, and beautiful. This is the way God transforms humans over the course of time.

Neuroplasticity

You may have heard the term "neuroplasticity." Neuroplasticity is the ability to change your brain structure based on the pathways you create through specific (and repetitive) actions, which create and strengthen neural connections. Neuroplasticity teaches us that whatever we think about most will grow. This applies to both positive and negative mental changes. When pastors like me talk about spiritual rhythms, we are referring to developing repetitive neural connections that change your brain structure, thus renewing your mind at the molecular level. This is why frequent Scripture intake, an intentional prayer life, and other routinized spiritual practices matter. These Christian practices reinforce truth and help us live faithfully to enact the gospel in the world.

Consider the following way of thinking about spiritual change in Romans 8:5–8:

> Those who live [or who act repetitively in ways that strengthen neural pathways] according to the flesh have their minds set on what the flesh desires; but those who live [or who act repetitively in ways that strengthen neural pathways] in accordance with the Spirit have their minds set on what the Spirit desires. The mind governed [what happens through repetition] by the flesh is death, but the mind governed [what happens through repetition] by the

Spirit is life and peace. The mind governed by the flesh is hostile to God; it does not submit to God's law, nor can it do so. Those who are in the realm of the flesh cannot please God.

The more we focus our minds on the flesh, the stronger those neural connections become, thus making those habits harder to break. For example, the more we look at pornography, use drugs and alcohol, gossip, or lie, the easier it becomes to keep doing it. When the habits of the flesh become more "natural" for us than the habits of the Spirit, we have become *malformed*. The goal of life is to become *transformed*, which means we must create habits that usher us into the life of the Spirit. Hence, Romans 8:9: "You, however, are not in the realm of the flesh but are in the realm of the Spirit, if indeed the Spirit of God lives in you. And if anyone does not have the Spirit of Christ, they do not belong to Christ."

To repeat, there is little formation without repetition. In these final chapters, we explore how the Holy Spirit seeks to work deeply through the brain in our breath, our stress, and our sleep. Each of these matters in relation to seeking a healthy spiritual life. Each of these can be improved through contemplative prayer. Let's dive in.

BREATH

Then the LORD God formed a man from the dust of the ground and breathed into his nostrils the breath of life, and the man became a living being.

—Genesis 2:7

Life is like a breath. We must be able to live in an easy rhythm between give and take. If we cannot learn to live and breathe in this rhythm, we will place ourselves in grave danger.

—David Steindl-Rast, *Gratefulness, the Heart of Prayer: An Approach to Life in Fullness*

YOU CAN GO ABOUT FORTY DAYS without food, a little under fourteen days without sleep, and four days at best without water. But you can hardly go four minutes without a breath. Breathing is everything. As goes your breathing, so goes your brain. And it's a good thing that oxygen is free, because if it wasn't we'd all go broke. On average, humans take 20,000 breaths each day. How many of those are you even conscious of taking? This chapter aims to help you connect the importance of breathing to brain coherence and, ultimately, to the renewing of our minds. Your breath feeds your brain (electrical current) and leads your heart (heart rhythm). But this all begins with God.

God's breath is better than good. According to the Bible, God's breath created what was deemed *very* good. This goes way beyond Colgate and Listerine. I'm talking about the divine breath of Yahweh (YHWH). In Genesis 2:7, the Scriptures record, "Then the LORD God formed a man from the dust of the ground and breathed into his nostrils the breath of life, and the man became a living being."

God originally breathed humankind into being. You. Me. Jackie Chan. Miles Davis. Cindy Lauper. All of us come from the mystical breath of the living God. Everything about us begins and ends with breath. Think about it. We mark our first moments on earth with breath. Upon delivering a baby, any good obstetrician checks the baby's vitals to ensure the child is breathing. This goes beyond the physical, it's spiritual too. The breath God breathes on us at the first creation is also the breath Jesus breathes on his disciples at the new creation (John 20:22). In every way imaginable, breath is life.

We mark our last moments on earth with breath too. As we gasp for one final drag of oxygen, our sacred lights go out. Breathing is a life essential. Everything about us begins and ends with breath.

If you live into your seventies, you will have taken over a billion breaths. The millions of breaths you will take—one after another—over a lifetime play a role in fueling the electrical current running through your brain. And that current fuels the neurons that make you, well, you. But for the electrical current to exist, it needs a generator, so to speak. Most people don't realize what that generator is.

So let's take a quiz. Adding the percentages up to 100 percent, guess what generates your life's energy:

Water   ___%
Diet   ___%
Sleep   ___%
Oxygen   ___%
TOTAL 100%

Water, diet, and sleep combined fuel only around 10 percent of your daily energy. What?! That means 90 percent of your energy every day—what makes you go—comes from oxygen, that is, breathing. And therein lies a problem. Our life rhythms don't mesh well with good breathing habits. This leads to stress on the heart and incoherence in the brain, which do not orient a life toward flourishing.

We often live lives hunched over a desk, with closed postures, and without appropriate exercise. Many people the world over live in places where air quality is poor. Low O_2 quantity combined with poor O_2 quality is a recipe for a short life. The lungs fail, the heart exhausts, and life cannot be sustained. Author and pastor Tricia McCary Rhodes writes:

> We may not realize how shallow our breathing is most of the time, largely because of the stress of life. This reduces the amount of oxygen to our brains, hindering our ability to concentrate. Shallow breathing also causes a buildup of carbon dioxide in our systems, which can create anxiety and disorientation. Deep breathing is, therefore, a cleansing act, dispelling toxins and calming our parasympathetic nervous system. The physiological effects of this alone can be powerful—from lowering or stabilizing blood pressure to diminishing the symptoms of heart disease or asthma. Beyond that, deep breathing increases our mental alertness and cognitive processing.[1]

Life can seem out of control. But check out what we can control:

By breathing more slowly, we can calm existing anxiety.
By breathing more deeply, we can create cognitive clarity.
By breathing more intentionally, we can gain brain energy.

But we seldom breathe as God intended. Instead, our breathing habits are fast and shallow, hurrying us along from one agenda to the next. Literally and figuratively, we can't catch our breath. Furthermore, we rarely allow ourselves the space to take a breath. It is no wonder we feel locked in lives of stress, fatigue, and incoherence.

When we breathe deeply, we have more energy to power our brains and bodies. This is like clean energy. Before Edison and Tesla, there was (and is) God, who both breathed us into existence and gives us the ability to breathe to sustain our lives. But a long and healthy life requires deep breaths.

I seldom compare the brain to a computer, but the metaphor is sometimes helpful. If the brain is the *hardware*, then the mind is the *software*. When the brain gets a healthy supply of oxygen, the mind can function at optimal levels, which helps with coherence, creativity, and mental health. But instead of taking deep breaths, we often take shallow breaths. We also sleep poorly and eat badly. This all adds up to the brain generating unclean electrical current, which partly explains our experience of brain fog, fatigue, and other symptoms of unhealth.[2] Conversely, clean current helps us think well and deeply. Life coherence all begins with breathing deeply.

Do you pause daily to breathe deeply?

In Sync

Here is how electrical current in the brain works. Electrical current travels from one neuron to another. In between the two neurons is a synaptic cleft that the current travels along, thus connecting the two neurons. The cleft is a space of about 20 to 40 nanometers. Yes, nanometers. When two neurons connect, they form a neural pathway. The more times two neurons connect, the stronger the pathway between them becomes. Oxygen from breath fuels much of this process.

The nervous system tells the other fourteen systems in the body what speed they need to go. When we worry, the brain moves into overdrive and works faster than it may need to. Essentially, the brain is the pedal that makes all the other systems go. When our breathing is poor, the brain sees this as stress, and the body produces chemicals to respond to the threat. So if our nervous system is off, it signals the rest of the body to be off. Over time, this causes chronic disease, inflammation, and so on because our adrenal glands are changing, our immune system is changing, our digestive system is changing, and our skin is changing.

Many live in sustained stress each day and are running their lives into the ground. If their breathing is shallow, their heart beats faster and thus works harder. Remember, everything is connected. So the better you breathe, the better your heart will be. Your heart takes its beating cues from your breathing. Good breaths make healthy hearts. Unfortunately, the inverse is also true.

Syncing our heart rate and our breathing is one of the things we seek to accomplish in contemplative prayer. If we can't sync our own selves, how will we sync with God, others, and creation? God created us to be in alignment with the grain of the universe. Each morning I challenge myself to begin within and aim to carry into every aspect of life that way of living with the grain of the universe.

The idea is that we are created to be in sync—not the boy band but a full integration of body, soul, and mind. Likewise, we are meant to be in sync with God, one another, and creation. All of this is woven into the fabric of our anatomy. Our lives were designed for harmony. But what often happens is just the opposite. Our breathing and heart rate get out of sync. Our relationships are shrouded in conflict and division. Our relationship to creation can be neglected and our intimacy with God ignored. Everything begins and ends with breath.

Speaking of congruence and integration, have you heard of the vagus nerve? This long nerve runs from the brain to the colon. Among many things, it serves to regulate relaxation and rest in the heart and lungs. Charles Stone writes, "Eighty percent of the fibers in this nerve runs from our internal organs (our belly, heart, lungs, and intestines) to the back of our brain. So, breathing is a way we can train our arousal system and minimize problems that come from unchecked anger, depression, and anxiety. Slow, focused breathing literally calms our minds and bodies."[3]

Remember those Lamaze classes for childbirth? We've known for some time now that regulating breath yields all sorts of health benefits.

A good breath takes about a four- to six-second intake of O_2, pauses at the top, then slowly releases CO_2. When exhaling, consider drawing your stomach muscles in tightly to squeeze the remaining CO_2 out of your lungs. Doc tells me that most humans fail to fully empty their lungs throughout the day. This means yesterday's CO_2 may still be sitting in the bottom third of your lungs. That is toxic and will wreak havoc on your health.

I'm not suggesting that every breath of your day look like this. But do you have times in the day when you pause and collect yourself? Do you ever stop to breathe well when facing a stressful moment or urgent decision? Or perhaps upon arriving home after a long day? Rather than turning on the television or checking in with social media, pause for several minutes and just inhale the breath that God freely gives you. A good place to begin is to pause three times per day to breathe eight deep breaths. Doing so will regulate your heartbeat and send peace through your soul. This will occur because of a decrease in cortisol levels in your brain, which will bring your heart back to rhythm.

Let's review. Your breath affects your brain, and your brain tells the rest of your body what to do. Life always begins and ends with breath.

Doc works a lot with professional athletes. He told me something fascinating about a player with the Los Angeles Clippers. According to NBA rules, a player attempting a free throw can toss the ball back to the referee one time before he has to shoot the free throw. Now, remember that inhaling deeply increases brain coherence. When we inhale deeply, our pupils constrict, periphery distractions are blocked, and our capacity to focus increases. So

Doc encouraged the Clippers player to take as much time as he could before shooting a free throw in order to breathe deeply so as to constrict his pupils and thus enhance his focus. It has been scientifically proven that deep breathing increases the accuracy of the free throw, and the player may hope it will lead to a larger contract in due time. The same dynamic is true for hitting a golf ball off the tee or shooting a rifle toward a target.

Breathing is also essential to prayer. When we pray, we should breathe deeply and slowly. This practice resets our brain chemistry, calms our bodies, and enhances our capacity to live in the present moment. Breath created us, and breath sustains us. Part of learning to pray involves (re)learning to breathe. A woman in my church recently wrote to tell me that when she was struggling to breathe while in the hospital with COVID symptoms, she breathed the Jesus Prayer ("Lord Jesus Christ, have mercy on me") for hours. She reported that it not only calmed her emotions but helped regulate her heart rhythm, quelling the fear she was carrying about the future. Praying and breathing go hand in hand.

Alveoli for Six Hundred Million, Alex

Permit me to invite you to learn a new and exciting word: alveoli (pronounced al-VEE-uh-lie). Alveoli are the tiny sacs on the surface of the lungs. The sacs catch O_2. Think of them like tiny catcher's mitts. As air comes into the lungs, the alveoli catch it and bring it in. There are six hundred million of these tiny sacs on a set of human lungs. If you were to stretch them out, they would cover the surface of a tennis court. Yes, a tennis court's worth of alveoli are covering your lungs right now! One of the reasons we must learn to breathe deeply—in and out—is because if our lungs are not empty, the alveoli cannot catch new O_2. When we exhale deeply, the alveoli can receive the next inhale of O_2, which is delivered to the brain. A good supply of oxygen increases coherence, life expectancy, imagination, and creativity. There is only an upside to breathing better. So why don't we? Because we are socially conditioned to lead lives of hurry, worry, and rush.

Be sure to catch the spiritual meaning behind alveoli, because it is easy to miss. We must empty if we are going to be filled. Augustine said it best: "We must empty ourselves of all that fills us so that we may be filled with what we are empty of."[4] Physically and spiritually, God supplies the necessary O_2 but invites us to exhale the CO_2. Our flourishing requires a beautiful partnership with God. Metaphorically speaking, God is the one who supplies spiritual O_2 in the form of grace and mercy. But we must do our part to confess and repent of the CO_2 in our lives that often remains somewhere deep within.

Consider this final nugget. The Gospels provide us with a glimpse of Jesus's first breaths from a cave in Bethlehem. They also provide us with information about his last moment before death. The Gospel writer Mark records that with a loud cry, Jesus breathed his last. The Gospel writers understood all too well that everything begins and ends with breath.

◆ PRACTICE ◆

Marc Dingman, author of *Your Brain, Explained*, writes, "Deep breathing, mindfulness meditation, and other relaxing techniques can be used before or during fear-inducing events to maintain composure in your body. This will make it more likely you can achieve a state of tranquility in your mind."[5]

The idea is to practice contemplative prayer in the calm of the day (such as first thing in the morning, before lunch, or at bedtime) so that when a stressful situation arises, your neural pathways have been formed in such a way that prayer becomes the natural response. When we live this way, we can control our breath and thus better regulate our heart rate and the release of chemicals in the brain. Sometimes those chemicals are necessary, but often we are better off breathing deeply and stepping back from a situation rather than giving in to fear, stress, and worry.

Find a comfortable place to sit and take only six breaths per minute, connecting your inhale and exhale with the Jesus Prayer below. Repeat this for five minutes. This activity will relax your mind and create space for increased peace, surrender, and trust in God.

Inhale: *Lord Jesus Christ*
Exhale: *Have mercy on me*

STRESS

The LORD will fight for you; you need only to be still.
　　　　　　　　　　　　　　　　　　—Exodus 14:14

Chronic stress even shrinks parts of our brains, especially areas involved in memory, and it grows the part of our brains behind fear and anxiety.
　　　　　—Armita Golkar et al., "The Influence of Work-Related
　　　　　　　　　Chronic Stress on the Regulation of Emotion
　　　　　　　　　and on Functional Connectivity in the Brain"

IN 2007, in a subway station in Washington, DC, renowned violinist Joshua Bell conducted an experiment on the adverse relationship between hurry and beauty. With his three-hundred-year-old instrument, he played six full pieces in public lasting forty-three minutes. At thirty-eight minutes into the performance, cameras had captured 1,097 people who had entered the station that day, yet only seven people had stopped to listen to Bell's music. Only seven had noticed the beauty freely emitting forth into the air. Can you guess the age demographic of those people?

They were children. It was the children who noticed what the adults were prone to miss.

Picasso is attributed as saying, "Every child is an artist. The problem is how to remain an artist once we grow up." Growing up today often implies an immunity to wonder, beauty, and what Charles Stone refers to as "holy noticing."[1] Maybe this is one of the reasons Jesus calls us to become like children lest we miss the kingdom of God at play all around us.

Evelyn Underhill once wrote that "the people of our time are . . . distracted . . . unable to interpret that which is happening, and full of apprehension about that which is to come."[2] In our stress, we stay busy. We rush. We hurry. We are like rocks being skipped swiftly along the surface.

Accustomed to roaring applause, Bell was met that day in that metro station not by the clapping of hands but by the sound of frenetic Oxfords and high heels. When did you last stop to listen to the music? There is beauty all around us if we choose to notice. Unfortunately, we often remain locked in our stress, living an unsustainable lifestyle at an unsustainable pace.

But this isn't the way life has to be. We have agency to choose new ways forward and not merely swallow whole the script that society has given us. Being with God is a part of the journey toward shalom.

Feierabend

The Germans have a unique term: Feierabend.[3] I haven't a clue how to pronounce all those consecutive vowels, but the concept deeply resonates. Feierabend is the intent to establish essential balance in life, to create clear distinctions between work and the rest of life. Feierabend invites workers to leave work in every sense when they step away from their place of employment. When we arrive home, we shouldn't still be solving work problems in our heads. The other parts of our lives deserve full attention, and so do we.

The Feierabend dynamic is beautiful but was complicated during a pandemic when many relocated the office to their home. While many saved time by not commuting, they lost the distinction between work life and the rest of life.

Studies have shown that when the work-life balance becomes blurred, overall life satisfaction diminishes and stress increases. When we are at work, we think about being with loved ones, and while with loved ones, we think about work.[4] Perhaps this explains the perception of German efficiency. When Feierabend is correctly implemented, we are more efficient at work because we are fully present to the work before us. Therefore, we get more done while working and can depart the office or factory or construction site in every way when the workday is done.

I conceived the idea for this book before the COVID-19 pandemic. But I wrote the book in the midst of it. I've no clue what the world will feel like by the time you read this. But this I do know: whether working at home or away from home, we must be intentional about creating this work-life separation.

Amygdala versus Prefrontal Cortex

The brain has three main sections: the stem, the cerebellum, and the cerebrum. Deep in the cerebrum are two amygdala that serve as an alarm system. These two small, almond-shaped areas are the "feeling" center, which "kick-starts the stress response and tags memories connected to emotion."[5] This is the "threat detector" or autopilot part of the brain, where fight-or-flight sensors are located. This part of the brain can save us from danger but can also cause all sorts of interpersonal problems when we let it run wild.[6] When you think amygdala, think emotions.

The prefrontal cortex, which is a part of the frontal lobe of the cerebrum, is responsible for cognitive reasoning and moderates social behavior. It's what helps us figure out life's complexities through the process of rational thought. According to author

Frank Lynn Meshberger, "The frontal lobes, above almost every part of the brain, are what make human beings human. The frontal lobes help us with our executive functions, help us plan our day, help us to organize our thoughts and behaviors, and help us to be compassionate to others."[7]

Returning to the amygdala, each one contains between ten and twelve million neurons. More neural pathways travel from the amygdala to the frontal lobe of the brain than the other direction. Truly, our emotions travel faster than the speed of consciousness.

So what does this mean? The amygdala sends us signals about life circumstances faster than the reasoning part of the brain. This explains why we react unduly in certain situations that feel threatening or overwhelming, then later regret reacting that way. When we react too fast in a situation, it is often the amygdala running the show. Our emotional response may save our life if we encounter a bear in the woods, but it often gets us in trouble with others if we are not disciplined enough to bring the prefrontal cortex to the party. When we react without thinking, we make snap judgments, we speak quickly, and before we know it, we are in debates with half of the people we know. News outlets and social media often target the amygdala and not the prefrontal cortex. This is because fear, which is an emotion moderated by the amygdala, is a much more efficient and effective target than critical reasoning.

Six emotions are associated with the amygdala: fear, shame, anger, disgust, sadness, and hopelessness. The prefrontal cortex generates forgiveness, empathy, listening, and self-control. So don't miss this. When we bypass the prefrontal cortex and live primarily from the amygdala, we exclude some of the most meaningful ways we are called to be human. Joshua Greene, professor of psychology at Harvard University, believes that less than 10 percent of the population uses the prefrontal cortex of their brain on a daily basis and that it is theoretically possible for one to go their entire life without using it.[8] This data indicates that stress is causing us to avoid using areas of the brain that God intended to be used for everyday life. That, I think, is a cause for deep lament and a recommitment to being with God.

Thirty-Eight Is Great?

At age thirty-eight, I began to notice my body changing. My joints ached more than usual. My muscles frequently tightened. My lower back was sore simply getting out of bed. For the first time, I realized the sobering fact we subconsciously suppress—but must eventually face: if we live long enough, age happens.

After pastoring for nearly two decades, the years of sermon writing, budget cycles, relentless reading, pastoral care, challenging decisions, and staff leadership had taken their toll. My mind said, "Keep going," while my body screamed, "Slow down!" I called Doc and told him something felt wrong. He put me through a battery of tests to diagnose the problem. The results? Adrenal fatigue. Psychiatrist and bestselling author Bessel Van der Kolk was right: the body keeps the score.[9]

Eventually, life and the stress of life catch up to us. Up to 60 percent of doctor visits today are due to stress-related issues.[10] According to psychology researcher Armita Golkar, "Chronic stress even shrinks parts of our brains, especially areas involved in memory, and it grows the part of our brains behind fear and anxiety."[11] Another certified neurology expert told me that when humans settle into low-hum stress as a new normal, the neurons in the amygdala—the emotional center—extend, while the neurons in the hippocampus—associated with forming new memories and much of daily life function—shrink. This means that our focus and function throughout the day weaken. This chain reaction means memory loss, adrenal fatigue, and increased blood sugar.

Many now realize that stress can actually kill us. Medical research reports that stress directly impacts one's life span. You're likely aware of the pressure it puts on the human heart, but stress also breaks down cellular development, causing degeneration in many body functions.[12] At the ends of our chromosomes are structures called telomeres. The more stress we take on in life, the more these telomeres shrink. This dynamic shortens the length of one's life span. When we learn to manage stress well, the telomeres remain intact.

One study of men in their thirties showed that the greatest threats to one's life span are smoking and diabetes (both reducing life span by approximately six years), followed by stress (reducing life span by approximately three years).[13]

Put into context:

That's over 1,000 days of quality life lost.

That's over 24,000 hours of potential conversations with dear friends lost.

That's over 86,400,000 seconds of potentially joyful moments with loved ones lost.

Birthdays, holidays, dinners, hiking, the list goes on and on. So much lost over so much stress. That's a big deal. We are killing ourselves.

Let's recall the word "absurd" from part 1. The word comes to us from the Latin word *sardus*, which means "deaf." We allow much of our lives to be absurd. Why? Because we choose to remain deaf (*sardus*) to the many ways we allow cultural values to slowly kill us.

From the epicenter of our stress, God invites us to slow down, breathe, reevaluate, and consider whether or not the burdens we carry are ours to bear. From that place of calm, we can more clearly discern if much of our stress is self-induced and if we are entangled in matters that are actually beyond our control.

I've noticed in my own life that much of the anxiety I carried over the past years resulted from circumstances I could not control. So often we stress over things that are beyond our ability to change. It's astonishing how much of life is beyond our control.

In my mind, I would play out endless conversations and scenarios, and for what? At what cost? My health, my mood with others, my emotional availability as a father, my sleep, my diet . . . the list goes on. But make no mistake, the body keeps the score.

A Very Stressful Time

I've always considered myself an avid reader. But after COVID-19 hit, I didn't have the capacity to read deeply for months. For me, stress manifests most in brain fog and fatigue. And these stress effects led to depression because I felt like a failure in life. I couldn't get out and felt hopeless not knowing what to do. Marc Dingman writes, "Depression can be just about as bad for you as smoking in terms of its ability to shorten your life."[14] I wasn't ready to die because of the stress I was experiencing. I hope you aren't either.

Chronic stress—even at low levels—diminishes our capacity to flourish. And the problem is that many of us do not feel we have the time to step back and evaluate whether or not we are living in a state of chronic stress. Moreover, many of us feel that even if this is the case, there is little we can do about it.

Our ancestors were accustomed to facing crises, whether it was a food crisis, war, a health crisis, or something else. Facing a crisis is nothing new in human history. But in 2020, the whole world faced not one crisis but many crises simultaneously. The number of crises faced at once is what made 2020 so incredibly stress-laced. Consider what we faced:

health fears
loss of loved ones
financial insecurity
job loss
diminishing retirements
social inequality

racialized violence and unrest
political chaos
educational shifts

Need I go on?

And with these crises came the onslaught of stress, anxiety, fear, distrust, and rage. Facing multiple crises at the same time is overwhelming, to say the least. Our minds are racing. Our hearts are exhausted. Our creativity is depleted. Our passions are numb.

We long for peace, but we do not yet know the way of being with God, a God who is the great anchor in the midst of an ever-expanding, always changing universe.

Holy Noticing

Maybe at this point you are thinking, "AJ, I'd like to find peace in my being and all that stuff, but life's demands do not afford me the luxury to slow down and be still." To that rebuttal, I plead (with a significant amount of pastoral empathy), "You can't afford not to slow down and be still."

This gentle invitation reminds me of a saying attributed to Martin Luther: "I have so much business, I cannot go without spending three hours daily in prayer."[15] Being with God (i.e., contemplative prayer) is what is most needed in this cultural moment. Stress is literally killing us. If it means you fail at some of life's imposing demands because you are seeking to gain peace and a longer life, then so be it.

Contemplative prayer helps us train our brains not to over-react, as much of society is accustomed to doing. In this form of prayer, we practice each day what it means to go slow, take time, and pray through life circumstances before reacting. Over time, being with God cultivates patience and compassion. Further, it permits the Holy Spirit groaning within us to be involved in our daily decisions. Contemplative prayer isn't merely a good idea; it's essential to navigating life well. I've included specific examples about how this works in the conclusion.

◆ PRACTICE ◆

We cannot change what we will not name. This is a concept I employed in my previous book, *The Enneagram for Spiritual Formation*. The concept also applies here, as we will rarely grow if we aren't honest about the ways we are carrying life's demands. One of the reasons we are often unaware of stress is that we do not slow down enough to check in with our bodies, our emotions, and our cognitive patterns. Being with God helps us do all three. So let's practice.

- Set a timer for seven minutes.
- Sit in a comfortable place with both feet on the floor.
- Become aware of your body slowly from your head all the way to your toes.
- Take notice if there is twitching, soreness, or any bodily sensations that are perhaps informing you of stress.
- Ask God for wisdom about what is being stored in your body.
- Attempt to specifically name what you are concerned or anxious about.
- Offer whatever stress you are feeling to God.
- Trust that Christ is willing to receive that stress and offer you lightness and liberation in return.
- Pray the Jesus Prayer, connecting it with your breath.

> Inhale: *Lord Jesus Christ*
> Exhale: *Have mercy on me*
> (Repeat)

SLEEP

So the LORD God caused the man to fall into a deep sleep; and while he was sleeping, he took one of the man's ribs and then closed up the place with flesh. Then the LORD God made a woman from the rib he had taken out of the man, and he brought her to the man.

—Genesis 2:21–22

We are the only animal on the planet that willingly resists sleep.

—Dr. Timothy Royer

I'M GRATEFUL for the good work of Charity: Water, a non-profit that aims to eliminate thirst in the world. I'm also grateful for their office space in downtown Manhattan. On Wednesday mornings back in 2011, the organization generously opened its doors for a weekly gathering of about one hundred men. The informal group nicknamed themselves "legends." The idea was that these men determined to become the kinds of humans their grandchildren would one day describe as legendary in the faith.

Men from all five boroughs would pour through the slender office doors and ascend in the elevator to congregate for an hour before shuffling off to work. Guest speakers were arranged to inspire men with Christian conviction to live meaningfully in a culture of confusion, self-indulgence, and misguided priorities. It was deeply successful, and as a pastor in the city, I was always grateful to eavesdrop.

But on one particular morning, a famous pastor had flown in and offered a challenge on "crushing it." For reasons I then could not articulate, his words did not resonate in my spirit. At the end of the talk, an exhausted twentysomething who had recently moved to the city and was comprehensively drained from the work hustle lifted his hand seeking clarity and insight, asking, "Pastor, how do I structure my life rhythms to be healthy and not burn out?"

The pastor paused, reflected, and then responded, "Sleep is for the dead. We need to stay awake as much as we can and push the limits. I'll sleep when I die."

The men collectively mustered a halfhearted cheer in response. But deep inside my soul, I cried for these men. This was terrible advice. Sleep is not the enemy. Sleep is a part of the waking life. Without good sleep, we cannot live a good waking life, because all of life was designed with rhythm baked in.

Resisting Sleep

Prior to the 1900s, the average human slept around nine hours per night. Currently, we sleep fewer than seven hours per night. To optimize long-term health and well-being, most neuroscientists recommend just over eight hours per night. When we get less than that, detriments to our health will eventually set in such as cardiovascular disease, type 2 diabetes, obesity, and hormone imbalance, to name a few. Based on age and stage, here is the amount of sleep some of our current medical scientists recommend:

Newborns: 14 to 17 hours
Infants: 12 to 15 hours
Toddlers: 11 to 14 hours
Preschoolers: 10 to 13 hours
Elementary schoolers: 9 to 11 hours
Teenagers: 8 to 10 hours
Young adults to adults: 7 to 9 hours
Older adults: 7 to 8 hours[1]

In many sectors of corporate culture, sleep deprivation is a badge of honor. When it comes to sleep, our culture is sick. What kind of culture incentivizes and celebrates defying the way God made us? Reflecting years later on the poor advice offered to young New Yorkers, I wondered, *What are the cultural values that drive us to sacrifice sleep and that would inspire a minister to encourage such reckless stewardship of the body?*

First, we live in a society that encourages *productivity* above all else. When output is one's primary reason for existence, all sorts of breakdowns ensue. Second, ours is a *merit-based* culture. We believe the lie that we must earn our worth, prove we are somebody. Naturally, doing so often requires that we burn the candle at both ends. Third, the illusion of *constructed identity* leads us to believe that identities are achieved rather than received. One of the greatest innovations of the Christian worldview is that God calls us beloved before we do anything. Reclaiming this reality every morning before my day begins creates a freer place from which to live. Fourth, our *technological addictions* allow us to resist the natural rhythms at every moment of the day. How many times do you find yourself beginning and ending your day on a screen, in bed? When blue light from devices habitually streams into our eyeballs upon waking and before sleeping, we can be sure that sleep deprivation is bound to set in.[2]

The Science of Sleep

Rejecting the sleep culture—or lack thereof—that exists in many corporate sectors, many athletes are waking up to the ancient way of healthy sleep. They are doing this because neuroscientists like Doc are helping them realize the science of sleep, which has much to do with the spirituality of sleep.

Athletes have recently discovered that they need good sleep habits in order to operate at an optimal level. The best and fastest way to increase athletic performance is sleeping for over eight hours every night. Studies show that athletes become stronger, faster, and make better decisions when they engage in healthy sleep rhythms.

Roger Federer once claimed that he can't play tennis well if he doesn't get enough sleep. He said, "If I don't sleep eleven to twelve hours per day, it's not right. If I don't have that amount of sleep, I hurt myself."[3] Why would he hurt himself if he didn't sleep that long? The answer is testosterone. Testosterone production is connected to good sleep. The better and longer one sleeps, the more testosterone one produces, and testosterone helps athletes withstand injuries.

Doc said that when it comes to NBA players, their brain scans can predict whether they will be prone to injury. Healthy brains result from good sleep, because both your brain and your body heals and recovers while sleeping. In fact, Doc told me that after assessing more than four hundred NBA athletes, he found that the number one contributor to performance over the long haul was sleep. Yet not all sleep is created equal.

Types of Sleep

What is college for? There are perhaps as many answers to that question as there are people. One of the reasons college exists is so people can try things they'd never try in their forties. At least, that's what my college buddy David thought. He and another friend agreed to a competition to see who could cheat sleep the longest. I love sleep, so I didn't go anywhere near this quest for sleep deprivation champion.

By the way, did you know that if you were to resist sleep for seven days, you would become completely out of touch with reality? The technical word for this is "psychotic." By day thirteen, you would die.

David won the competition. He stayed awake for over forty hours. When he did, finally, decide to sleep, he confessed that he felt physically sick and that it took his body days to recover. Sleep is a gift we surrender to, not an obligation we endure.

There are three primary ways to sleep. Think about which best describes your sleep habits. The first is referred to as sleep debt. Sleep debt describes the habit of most Americans. If you fall asleep in under seven minutes of going to bed, you most likely have sleep debt, meaning the body is overly weary and you may not be getting the quality of rest necessary for flourishing. Doc says the fancy term for this is "sleep latency disorder." Many people brag about sleeping when they "hit the pillow." This might feel nice, but it's not a good way to function in the long term.

Then there are those who struggle to fall asleep. Perhaps you are exhausted for parts of the day, then struggle to sleep when the time comes. If it takes you more than thirty minutes to fall asleep, you may be experiencing primary insomnia. This is not extreme insomnia popular in novels but a form that people like me wrestle with frequently.

The third form of sleep is circadian rhythm. This is how we are created to sleep. If you fall asleep between seven and twenty minutes, it's a good indication that your life is in healthy circadian rhythm. This is what we are aiming for when we seek to flourish.

Circadian Rhythm

In a recorded conversation I had with Doc, he told me, "You cannot choose to stay up until the wee hours of the night looking at a screen and then get ten hours of sleep, wake up after lunch, and have the same level of rest and clarity as someone who went to bed at 10 p.m. and awoke at 6 a.m. What you are doing is out of alignment with the rhythm God has designed, which is this big thing in the sky we call the sun. The sun sets us up to be in circadian rhythm."

Humans were designed to be in sync with the earth's twenty-four-hour rotation. When we work against the sun, our bodies do not respond correctly, because sunlight is the cue for much of what is happening in our brains. Even though some people may have to work the night shift, their bodies never fully adjust to it because we aren't meant to work during those hours. So if you are a night owl who is prone to sleep in, you may want to reconsider if you care deeply about creativity, optimization, and mental clarity.

I'll try to keep this simple but meaningful at the same time. Our bodies consume energy all day long. From the chapter on breath, you may recall the electrical current in the brain. We measure that current with an EEG. Our hearts, too, run on electricity. We measure that current with an EKG. When we sleep, our bodies, which have consumed energy all day, go into what is called a parasympathetic state in which we renew, restore, and regenerate energy for the next day. Simple enough.

Here is where the importance of circadian rhythm comes in. All the chemicals in the brain are controlled by a twenty-four-hour rhythm that is regulated by sunlight. Adrenaline (in the form of cortisol) makes us wake. Melatonin makes us sleep. Melatonin is released in the brain when the sun goes down. When the sun sets, our brains, designed by God with circadian rhythm in mind, start to produce melatonin to make us sleep. This phenomenon helps explain why it is harmful to look at screens before bed. They release blue light, which confuses the brain into thinking it is daytime, thus suppressing melatonin production and making it difficult for us to fall asleep.

Peak melatonin production happens at midnight, which co-incides with the time of the deepest stage of sleep. Midnight is the darkest time of the twenty-four-hour period, which explains why the most melatonin is released around that time. Conversely, adrenaline (cortisol), which makes us wake, peaks in production when the sun rises around 7 a.m. This chemical release is what wakes us up. Amazing!

Let's dig deeper. First thing every morning, your body releases eight units of cortisol. By noon, your cortisol level has dwindled to around three units. At sunset, your body should be functioning at around two units. At bedtime—around 10 p.m.—there should be around one unit of cortisol in your system, which then triggers your brain to produce melatonin because it's now time to sleep. In order to trigger melatonin release, your body must get below one unit of cortisol.

Although science backs up these claims, science did not establish them; the Scriptures did. Both the Old and New Testaments affirm that creation came into existence with a natural order. A human must rest for, at minimum, eight hours within a twenty-four-hour period in order to regenerate. A human should rest for a full twenty-four-hour period at least once a week, which is what we call sabbath. Suffice it to say, God created the earth with the intent that rest is a significant part of the equation. It's just that we live in a society that doesn't really care about science and spirituality enough to believe it.

"Sleep" Is a Terrible Term

If I were to ask you, "What did you do yesterday?" and you were to respond, "I was awake," I'd be like, "Duh." Such a vague answer would be inadequate. In fact, I would probably assume you were being standoffish or sarcastic. In truth, so many things happen during a day that the answer "I was awake" simply doesn't cover them all. The same is true about sleep. So many things happen and so many things are accomplished while we sleep. Sleep is brilliant. Sleep is not merely a neutral state of rest and recovery. Sleep is incredibly productive.

Check this out. During the first four hours of sleep, the brain goes to work restoring the body. So muscles, organs, and so on all get the brain's focus so they can heal themselves. During the last four hours, the brain heals itself. When these latter hours kick in, we experience all sorts of emotions and problem solving, but the body is paralyzed in this state. We often refer to this as dreaming. You may know this state of sleep as REM, for rapid eye movement.

But here is why sleep is so brilliant. Have you ever gone to bed with an unsolved problem only to unlock the answer to that problem the next morning? When this happens, it's because the brain was at work when you were asleep solving problems and sorting out the universe. What?! If you have a dilemma right now, it is possible that the solution you seek will not be discovered through fighting sleep to work out the problem. It is possible that the right answer will come only after you've given your brain time to work on it while you're sleeping. I cannot tell you how many dots get connected in my life when I'm taking a shower in the morning. This is partly because I have just woken from a sleep during which my brain has been working. So if you have issues like me, go to bed. I'm sure everyone will be glad.

Another brilliant and generative thing that REM sleep does for us is store memories. While we're sleeping, our brains file memories from short to long term so they can remain with us and help us navigate life.

These are some of the physiological aspects of good sleep. Now let's consider the spiritual aspect.

Sleep Is Spiritual

The Bible is rather positive about sleep. True, there is that one account when Jesus asks the disciples to stay awake with him and they don't. But aside from that, many incredible things take place in the context of humans sleeping.[4]

- Adam is in a deep sleep while Eve is formed from him.
- Abram is in a deep sleep while God creates (and literally walks through) the covenant.
- Jacob's ladder occurs during sleep.
- Daniel dreams of the four beasts.
- An angel tells Joseph during a dream not to divorce Mary. Yeah, that's a big deal.
- Pilate's wife is given a revelation about Jesus through a nightmare.
- Possibly John's entire Revelation is imparted while he is sleeping.

These are just a few. Not only do our brains go to work physiologically while we sleep, but our God also goes to work on us while we sleep! Sleep is not a waste of time. Adequate sleep is powerful.

God does wonders in the dark. The task is to trust God's activity not only while we are awake but also while we are asleep. I'm an Anglican priest. One of the prayers my tradition invites people to pray before retiring for the day is this: "Guide me waking, O Lord, and guard me sleeping." This guarding does not mean God merely stoically watches over us as we surrender to the night. God guards us through active engagement with our neural pathways, realigning our imaginations toward the anticipation of the kingdom.

Hear me. I am not suggesting we indulge in naps and extended siestas and sleep our lives away. I am suggesting that in order for us to be our most creative, aware, and intelligent selves, we must arrange our lives in proper rhythm. And good sleep is a vital part of that rhythm.

In that same conversation I had with Doc, he asked me to imagine the brain as an investment. As previously stated, in the first four hours of sleep, our bodies recover. In the second four hours, our brains recover and we experience deep REM. Many people sleep four hours a day and think they are fully recovered. True, their bodies may feel restored, but over time, the long-term impact on their brain health will be detrimental. We can't cheat sleep and expect to flourish.

The first four hours get us through tomorrow. Our bodies can function, and many people go for long periods of time on four to five hours of sleep per night. Maybe that's you. The second four hours is the long-term investment toward brain health. We must think about long-term brain investment and aim to sleep over eight hours each night.

Something I find very interesting is that our brains constrict when we sleep in order to squeeze out the toxins and then flush them through our system. Our brains act like a kind of cranial toilet. This serves as a reminder of our daily need for spiritual healing. What is true for us physically is also true for us spiritually. It's the subtle whisper, "You are not a machine. You are human, and you need healing." When we fight sleep, we resist healing. Psalm 121:4 tells us that we serve a God who doesn't sleep. Our God goes to work on us while we sleep. Just as contemplative prayer is resting in God while awake, so quality sleep is a form of resting in God. God ministers to us in both states of life, which are passive and open to God's presence.

Sleep is spiritual. It is the daily practice of letting go; it is the daily reminder that we are human and not God. Sleep is a daily dying to one's self and the ego. Another term for sleep is "surrender."

Imagine sleep as the daily practice of surrendering to God—surrendering mind, emotions, and body. When you go to bed this evening, treat it as an act of spiritual surrender to a God who loves you. Perhaps say just before falling asleep, "Lord, I surrender to you. Heal me as I sleep." Or join me in praying the old prayer,

"Guide me waking, O Lord, and guard me sleeping." May you surrender well and awake restored.

◆ PRACTICE ◆

There is an Italian phrase *la dolce far niente*—"the sweetness of doing nothing." Michael Hyatt writes, "Americans usually feel guilty doing nothing. Our brains aren't designed to run nonstop. When we drop things into neutral, ideas flow on their own, memories sort themselves out, and we give ourselves a chance to rest. If you think about it, most of your breakthrough ideas in your business or personal life come when you're relaxed enough to let your mind wander. Creativity depends on times of disengagement, which means doing nothing from time to time is a competitive advantage."[5]

Perhaps your response to Hyatt is something like, "The spirituality of doing nothing might be good for Seinfeld but not for me. Time is money, life is hustle, neutral goes nowhere." But remember that all creation has a rhythm and that you are a part of that creation. Therefore, God designed you to be in rhythm with the created order. To resist sleep is to resist the created order. This will never lead to God's dream for you: shalom. Shalom is peace, harmony, wholeness, tranquility, completeness. Shalom is the result of living within God's created order.

Consider two ways to align yourself with God's created order:

1. Observe a twenty-four-hour sabbath. Design a day of enjoyment, delight, and rest.
2. Get eight to nine hours of quality sleep each night. Attempt to stop using technology that emits blue light two hours before retiring, and retire no later than 11 p.m. After one month of doing this, evaluate any differences in your energy and joy levels.

Maybe you're thinking, "AJ, this all sounds great. But my mind is racing when I hit the pillow. I'm stressed in so many ways. What can I do?"

This is a common sentiment. I said it myself to Doc. Doc replied, "Ask yourself, 'What would make a mushroom grow?'" (No, this is not a subversive endorsement for psychedelics.) Follow mushroom farming 101 to get your sleep cycle on track:

1. Make it dark. Turn off all the lights in the room, including the little blue lights on your devices. If you have the means, consider buying darkening shades. A dark environment slows down the brain and promotes melatonin release.

2. Make it moist. When the dry winter months set in, with a lack of moisture (low humidity), your respiratory system has to work overtime and can pull you out of sleep. A humidifier is helpful.

3. Make it cool. When the temperature is low, your body can sense that it is time for sleep. Some people put their thermostat below 60 degrees to create this optimal environment for sleeping. That setting can tax your AC in the hot summer months, but the colder the better when it comes to sleeping.

Rest deeply, my friend!

CONCLUSION

Benefits of Contemplative Prayer

THE AIMS of this book were threefold.

Part 1 sought to establish that Western culture tends toward absurd values such as hurry, anxiety, and chaos. Society then rebrands those values of absurdity, calling them "normal." This means that a contemplative orientation (e.g., stillness, silence, and solitude) is countercultural and will be viewed in society as a kind of "reverse absurdity." Therefore, Christ followers who prioritize and routinize being with God will be seen as absurdly wasting time.

Part 2 encouraged Christ followers to courageously get off the absurd merry-go-round of the West and presented a better way to be human. The contemplative path is not optional but essential to flourishing. It should also be essential, once again, to the practices of the local church. Being with God is of dire necessity. Within a culture of absurdity, this spiritual pathway is not innate but must be learned and practiced. If the church is going to survive the twenty-first century, it must move away from both the entertainment and the seeker model and instead form its members in ways that are countercultural.

The third part showed how a culture of technological absurdity is rewiring our neural pathways in all the wrong directions. Through poor breathing habits, increased stress, and unhealthy sleep patterns, we are slowly killing ourselves. Being with God is one of the ways we can restore our relationships with our own bodies, our loved ones, and the world.

These final words aim to highlight a few benefits of contemplative prayer within a culture of absurdity. One of the greatest critiques and misunderstandings of contemplative prayer is whether it "works." What critics mean by this is whether or not it produces any kind of effect. For example, when we worship God in cataphatic ways (through the senses), we feel many effects—such as the rush of dopamine when we lift our hands and sing. Or when we pray for healing, one might feel tingling in the body or heat in the hands. Many shed tears when touched deeply by a sermon, or the sacraments. These are all good manifestations of God's presence and are to be valued.

Yet the apophatic tradition (beyond the senses) should not be ignored. In one sense, being with God is, in itself, the goal. Even if nothing "happens," we can conclude that opening quiet space for the Lord to fill is reward enough. However, science is beginning to reveal other benefits of contemplative prayer.

Overcoming Addiction

In his book *Neurotheology*, Andrew Newberg cites a study of fMRI brain scans of those who had committed to contemplative prayer through their involvement with Alcoholics Anonymous: "The prayer practice was found to be associated with less alcohol craving and significant changes in the brain areas involved with self-referential processing and the default mode network. These results demonstrate how prayer can help a person control his or her attention and emotions, resulting in less craving and, hopefully, less return to alcohol misuse and abuse."[1]

We do not know exactly what is happening in the brain when we pray. But as with the sacraments, we can boldly proclaim that something *is* happening. This is the place where divine mystery comes in. We don't have to know everything, but we can know that we are known deeply by God and that the God who is present through the Holy Spirit's indwelling is at work within the core of our being.

When I pray over people who are experiencing addiction or are in need of healing of any kind, I make it a habit to ask the Spirit indwelling them to heal them from within. You see, our starting point within the body of Christ is that God is already present at the core of our being. We are not asking a God who dwells somewhere beyond Pluto to come and heal. Rather, sacred Scripture teaches that God is immanent and intimate. This means God is not only close but also love. The God who resides within us can minister to us from within our bodies and even while we sleep. This is profound, to say the least.

Healing from Trauma

Ours is an age in which people are no longer criticized for confessing traumatic experience. This is a good thing. I'd venture to guess that all humans have experienced trauma on some level. This is part of the broken condition we inherited in a fallen world. Studies of meditation report a possible connection between contemplative prayer and healing of trauma.[2]

More often than not, traumatic experiences manifest in various forms of depression. Newburg reports on the science of contemplative prayer, writing, "People with depression frequently have decreased brain activity in specific cortical regions. . . . [These regions] have been shown to be activated during meditation practices. In fact, studies have documented persistently increased activity and even increased brain thickness in these areas associated with long-term meditation practices. It might be inferred from such data that meditation has a very specific effect on brain function that can mitigate psychological disturbances."[3]

Many medical reports agree that meditation practices alter structures in the brain. These are not arbitrary structures but structures that are essential to healthy sensory, cognitive, and emotional processing.[4] Again, we do not know precisely what is happening, but we can say with conviction that prayer impacts the brain. When the mind is renewed, transformation is possible. As Christ followers, we believe this is the power of the Holy Spirit at work within us.

Cultivating Positive Traits

Daniel Goleman and Richard Davidson's book *Altered Traits* chronicles the journey of monks who cultivated lives of compassion through years of contemplative prayer. Their conclusion is that as cortical thickness in the brain increases through mindfulness practice, compassion and empathy are further developed.[5] This explains why the Western world isn't known for cultures of compassion. Slowing down and being still are not marketable values.

In just thirty hours of contemplative prayer over an eight-week stretch, one can begin to experience lessened reactivity in the amygdala (see chap. 11).[6] This means that when a stressful situation occurs, one has greater capacity to step back, evaluate, and not become entangled to the point of emotional overload. The aim isn't that we become stoic but rather that we become capable of less reactivity to various situations. This is one of the ways we grow the fruit of the Spirit called self-control. Lord knows our world needs more of that.

In the short term, being with God can help in the cultivation of empathy. It can also increase our ability to focus—for example, when studying for a real estate exam or the GRE. The encouragement here is that we don't have to be a yogi before we begin enjoying some of the benefits of contemplative prayer.

However, it is the long-term practice that produces the greatest transformation. This includes transformation of the human body. According to Goleman, "Small improvements in the molecular markers of cellular aging seem to emerge with just thirty hours of practice. Still, all such effects are unlikely to persist without sustained practice."[7] A commitment to regular, long-term contemplative prayer decreases the brain's production of cortisol, increases attention span, syncs the heart rate with breathing, and, according to Goleman, "shrinks the neural circuits of the nucleus accumbens associated with 'wanting' or attachment."[8] In an absurd culture of consumerism, being with God has incredible counter formation effects. With Psalm 23, we confess, "The LORD is my shepherd; I shall not want" (KJV). When we loosen our grip on Western values and trust the good Shepherd of our souls, holistic healing becomes possible.

Cooperating with God

Religion has a bad rap. People like spirituality but not religion. The issue is more complicated than we can explore in this book, but generally, spirituality is deemed as more authentic because it is more spontaneous and less systematized. Religion, on the other hand, is viewed as routine and more systematized. In an individualistic age that idolizes autonomy and individual expression, religion doesn't stand a chance. Christianity affirms both spontaneous spirituality and systematized religion. We need spontaneous spirituality through which God is at work wildly within us and the world. But we also need religion that can routinize and habituate our spiritual lives.

Newberg studied the difference that contemplative prayer makes for those who adhere to a form of religion compared to those who do not. His conclusions were compelling: "A brain scan study we performed on an atheist who meditated on the notion of God generally showed a brain that was unable to grasp that particular concept. This person's brain did not activate during the meditation practice like that of other people who truly believed in what they were meditating upon. Thus, there appears to be something to be said for fully 'buying into' the practices that you perform."[9]

Believing religious dogma, through faith, seems to impact the effects of prayer. I believe that faith opens us up for God to act freely within us. Faith in the New Testament is better translated as "trust," in my opinion. It appears that, at least at this time in God's history with us, God is unwilling to act in ways that violate our freedom. God looks for covenant partners who are desirous for God to act and move. There is great power in agreement. Religion helps us "agree" with God's radical and sanctifying movement within us.

Think of it like going to a chiropractor. Before cracking a patient's neck, the chiropractor always asks the patient to relax. What they are saying is, in effect, "Trust me." When we trust the person, relax, and allow them to freely practice their craft, the cracking goes much more smoothly. When we resist, the potential relief to the body decreases. It is much the same, I think, with religion and spirituality. When we pray, our trust in God to freely be God within us increases God's effect on our lives. Distrust and doubt limit the work God does in our lives. This doesn't mean that God is limited in any way but rather that he chooses to work inside the framework of freedom he imparted to us in Genesis 1–2. Hear me, my reformed friends: I am not here referring to the doctrine known as justification. I am referring mostly to the doctrine of sanctification. Sanctification demands human participation in cooperation with the Holy Spirit for optimal impact.

Conclusion (to the Conclusion)

Our world is absurd. Who could argue with that? What is absurd we now call "normal." Returning to the way God intended us to be human will be viewed as absurd, but it's necessary. I pray you will know the power and love of the living God—a God who is not "out there" somewhere waiting to be apprehended but a God who is willing and able to reside at the core of your being. May you fully surrender to this wild God who wants to rewire your neural pathways, heal your emotions, and empower you as a force of good in this beautiful and broken world.

Selah.

DESIGNING A CONTEMPLATIVE RETREAT

OVER THE YEARS, I have been grateful to lead dozens of contemplative retreats, guiding people gently into the waters of *being with God*. Having discovered a few things along the way, I'd like to pass along some of the insights should you desire to lead either a self-guided contemplative retreat or one for others to join you.

First of all, retreats are meant to be true to the name—retreat. People (including you) need to return from a retreat rested, refreshed, and reenergized. If a retreat is freighted with too much content and too little reflection time (both with self and others), people will be in danger of returning exhausted. So always make a retreat plan with the main purpose to rest—mind, body, and soul. Be sure that people get enough rest in the form of good sleep (eight hours minimum) and free time. Remember that people are diverse in personality (introvert/extrovert, for example), so design a schedule taking those nuances into consideration. I always give people choices for free time so that they can assess what they need and choose what is best for them.

Second, people need food, preferably good food. When I began taking New Yorkers away for retreats, we discovered a monastery where the food was on point. In fact, it was made by students at the Culinary Institute of America. So breakfast, lunch, and dinner not only were prepared for us but also were delicious and nutritious. Aim to find a location where eating is a valuable practice to experience together.

Third, assign content that will be discussed well in advance of the retreat. This will give those who attend time to read and reflect beforehand based on the availability of their schedules. If you want to schedule reading time while on the retreat so that the content is fresh in participants' minds, be aware that people process content at different levels and at different paces. So don't overload them with copious amounts of information.

Fourth, schedule guided conversations to combine teaching, conversation, and practice. People need guidance when starting the contemplative journey because it can be confusing and awkward. Because we live in a culture of absurdity (and are conditioned to call that way of life "normal"), people find being with God difficult. They need concise but compassionate instruction to help them along the path. They also need time to ask questions and create conversations together. Sometimes the best instruction on retreats I lead comes not from my teaching but from an insight someone else has that helps others along the path. So make space for good discussion where questions are welcomed and co-learning is permitted. At the beginning and/or the end of a group time, I suggest trying a practice together. For example, start with a brief *lectio divina* and then spend time talking about the experience before jumping into teaching. People need space and time to talk about what they are experiencing. Many times the learning process happens through practice. Before concluding a group session, consider ending the time with a contemplative prayer so the group can deeply rest in God's presence before leaving the room.

Fifth and finally, find a place that inspires and is restful. Dirty living spaces, uncomfortable beds, and environments that are too hot or too cold are not helpful. You want your people (including you) to rest well and feel at home away from home. Don't underestimate how important the environment is on a retreat. Try to find a place where people have their own bedroom and also access to nature. Good sleep and contact with creation are both ways God heals us.

If you are looking for content to discuss with prayer practices, the "Necessity" section of this book is helpful. If you are designing a retreat from a Friday evening to a Sunday morning, here is a suggested schedule for you to use.

Friday

5:00 p.m.—Arrival/check-in

6:00 p.m.—Dinner

7:00 p.m.—Session 1 (chap. 4, "Noise")
Welcome, discussion,[1] and practice[2]

8:30 p.m.—Evening prayer (compline)[3]

9:00 p.m.—The Great Silence[4]

Saturday

8:00 a.m.—Breakfast (in silence)

9:00 a.m.—Session 2 (chap. 5, "Room")
Teaching, discussion, and practice

10:30 a.m.—Free time

12:00 p.m.—Lunch

1:00 p.m.—Session 3 (chap. 6, "Still")
Teaching, discussion, and practice

2:30 p.m.—Free time

4:30 p.m.—Session 4 (chap. 7, "Groans")
    Teaching, discussion, and practice
6:00 p.m.—Dinner
7:00 p.m.—Session 5 (chap. 8, "Dive")
    Teaching, discussion, and practice
8:30 p.m.—Evening prayer
9:00 p.m.—The Great Silence

Sunday

8:00 a.m.—Breakfast (in silence)
9:00 a.m.—Session 6 (chap. 9, "Gaze")
    Teaching, discussion, and practice
10:30 a.m.—Depart

ADDITIONAL RESOURCES

Group Study

Bourgeault, Cynthia. *Centering Prayer and Inner Awakening.* Cambridge, MA: Cowley, 2004.

Rohr, Richard. *The Naked Now: Learning to See as the Mystics See.* New York: Crossroad, 2009.

Devotional Meditations

Claiborne, Shane. *Common Prayer: A Liturgy for Ordinary Radicals.* Grand Rapids: Zondervan, 2010.

Merton, Thomas. *New Seeds of Contemplation.* New York: New Directions, 2007.

Personal Equipping

Finley, James. *Merton's Palace of Nowhere.* 40th anniv. ed. Notre Dame, IN: Ave Maria, 2017.

Keating, Thomas. *Open Mind, Open Heart: The Contemplative Dimension of the Gospel.* New York: Continuum, 2006.

Laird, Martin S. *A Sunlit Absence: Silence, Awareness, and Contemplation.* New York: Oxford University Press, 2011.

Historical Perspectives

Holder, Arthur G. *Christian Spirituality: The Classics.* London: Routledge, 2009.

Sittser, Gerald Lawson. *Water from a Deep Well: Christian Spirituality from Early Martyrs to Modern Missionaries.* Downers Grove, IL: IVP Books, 2007.

NOTES

Introduction

1. Mark E. Thibodeaux, *Armchair Mystic: Easing into Contemplative Prayer* (Cincinnati: St. Anthony Messenger Press, 2001), 17.

2. Thibodeaux, *Armchair Mystic*, 17.

3. Carlo Carretto, *Letters from the Desert* (Maryknoll, NY: Orbis Books, 1972), locs. 270–71 of 1420. Kindle.

4. Thibodeaux, *Armchair Mystic*, 29.

5. M. Robert Mulholland Jr., *The Deeper Journey: The Spirituality of Discovering Your True Self* (Downers Grove, IL: IVP Books, 2006), 97.

6. Jonathan Sacks, ed. and trans., *The Koren Siddur* (New Milford, CT: Koren, 2009), xliv.

7. Jacopo Prisco, "Inside the World's Quietest Room," CNN, updated March 28, 2018, https://www.cnn.com/style/article/anechoic-chamber-worlds-quietest -room/index.html.

Part 1: Absurdity

1. Wayne Muller, *Sabbath: Finding Rest, Renewal, and Delight in Our Busy Lives* (New York: Bantam, 2000), 3.

2. M. Robert Mulholland Jr., *The Deeper Journey: The Spirituality of Discovering Your True Self* (Downers Grove, IL: IVP Books, 2006), 97.

Chapter 1: Weird

1. I also affirm the argument that there are many different ways to define the terms.

2. The desert fathers and mothers were Christian mystics and hermits who fled the cultural, watered-down Christianity emerging in the fourth century in order to cultivate Christlikeness through contemplative practice in the desert.

3. Henri J. M. Nouwen, *The Return of the Prodigal Son: A Story of Homecoming* (London: Darton, Longman & Todd, 2008), 13.

4. Basil the Great, "Letter 2 (to Gregory of Nazianzus)," trans. Roy J. Deferrari, Loeb Classical Library 190 (Cambridge, MA: Harvard University Press, 1926), 1.9.

5. Irina Ivanova, "World Health Organization Classifies Work 'Burnout' as an Occupational Phenomenon," CBS News, updated May 28, 2019, https:// www.cbsnews.com/news/world-health-organization-classifies-work-burnout -an-occupational-phenomenon-2019-05-28.

6. Rowan Williams, "To Be Fully Human Is to Be Recreated in the Image of Christ's Humanity," address to the Roman Synod of Bishops, Vatican City, October 11, 2012, https://zenit.org/articles/archbishop-rowan-williams-address -to-the-synod-of-bishops.

Chapter 2: Tech

1. Tali Sharot, *The Influential Mind: What the Brain Reveals about Our Power to Change Others* (New York: Henry Holt, 2018), 152.

2. Sharot, *Influential Mind*, 153.

3. Neil Postman, *Amusing Ourselves to Death: Public Discourse in the Age of Show Business* (New York: Penguin, 1985).

4. John Eldredge, *Get Your Life Back: Everyday Practices for a World Gone Mad* (Nashville: Thomas Nelson, 2020), loc. 1129 of 2699. Kindle.

5. Quoted in Rod Dreher, *The Benedict Option: A Strategy for Christians in a Post-Christian Nation* (New York: Penguin, 2018), 71.

6. Michael S. Hyatt, *Free to Focus: A Total Productivity System to Achieve More by Doing Less* (Grand Rapids: Baker Books, 2019), 15.

7. James K. A. Smith, "In Praise of Boredom," *Image*, no. 99, https://image journal.org/article/in-praise-of-boredom.

8. David Zahl, *Seculosity: How Career, Parenting, Technology, Food, Politics, and Romance Became Our New Religion and What to Do about It* (Minneapolis: Fortress, 2019), 78.

9. Quoted in Andrew B. Newberg and Mark Robert Waldman, *How God Changes Your Brain: Breakthrough Findings from a Leading Neuroscientist* (New York: Ballantine, 2010), 2.

10. Herbert A. Simon, "Designing Organizations for an Information-Rich World," in *Computers, Communication, and the Public Interest*, ed. Martin Greenberger (Baltimore: Johns Hopkins University Press, 1971), 40.

11. Samuel Wells, *Walk Humbly: Encouragements for Living, Working, and Being* (Grand Rapids: Eerdmans, 2019), 66.

Chapter 3: Hear

1. National Geographic Society, "Noise Pollution," *National Geographic*, last updated July 16, 2019, https://www.nationalgeographic.org/encyclopedia/noise-pollution.

2. National Geographic Society, "Noise Pollution."

3. Meg Selig, "What Did You Say?! How Noise Pollution Is Harming You," *Psychology Today*, September 25, 2013, https://www.psychologytoday.com/us/blog/changepower/201309/what-did-you-say-how-noise-pollution-is-harming-you.

4. United Nations Department of Economic and Social Affairs, "The Speed of Urbanization around the World," *Population Facts*, no. 2018/1, December 2018, https://population.un.org/wup/Publications/Files/WUP2018-PopFacts_2018-1.pdf.

5. Ron Chepesiuk, "Decibel Hell: The Effects of Living in a Noisy World," *Environmental Health Perspectives* 113, no. 1 (January 2005): A34–A41, https://www.ncbi.nlm.nih.gov/pmc/articles/PMC1253729.

6. Walter Yeates, "Noise in Cities: 11 Cities Exposed to Noise Pollution," *Krisp* (blog), June 20, 2020, https://krisp.ai/blog/noise-pollution-in-cities.

7. Hana Kusumoto, "Japanese Residents Awarded $7 Million over Military Aircraft Noise at Yokota," *Stars and Stripes*, June 7, 2019, https://www.stripes.com/news/pacific/japanese-residents-awarded-7-million-over-military-aircraft-noise-at-yokota-1.585018.

8. National Geographic Society, "Noise Pollution."

9. National Geographic Society, "Noise Pollution."

10. "Soundcheck: Ocean Noise," National Oceanic and Atmospheric Administration, December 1, 2016, https://www.noaa.gov/explainers/soundcheck-ocean-noise.

11. Eugene H. Peterson, *The Contemplative Pastor: Returning to the Art of Spiritual Direction* (Grand Rapids: Eerdmans, 1996), locs. 455–56 of 1463. Kindle.

12. Thomas Oden, *The Rebirth of Orthodoxy* (San Francisco: HarperSanFrancisco, 2003), 151.

13. Linda Stone, "Beyond Simple Multi-Tasking: Continuous Partial Attention," *Linda Stone* (blog), November 30, 2009, https://lindastone.net/2009/11/30/beyond-simple-multi-tasking-continuous-partial-attention.

Chapter 4: Noise

1. "005 Noise—Rob Bell—Nooma," YouTube video, 10:23, September 22, 2016, https://youtu.be/9XFoReR_XBE.

2. Rachel Emma Silverman, "Workplace Distractions: Here's Why You Won't Finish This Article," *Wall Street Journal*, December 11, 2012, https://www.wsj.com/articles/SB10001424127887324339204578173252223022388.

3. Arthur G. Holder, *Christian Spirituality: The Classics* (London: Routledge, 2009), 266.

4. Martin S. Laird, *A Sunlit Absence: Silence, Awareness, and Contemplation* (New York: Oxford University Press, 2011), 50.

5. Laird, *Sunlit Absence*, 56.

6. Daniel Goleman, *Focus: The Hidden Driver of Excellence* (New York: HarperCollins, 2013), 14.

7. Hesychios, *On Watchfulness and Holiness* 130, in *Philokalia*, vol. 1, trans. G. E. H. Palmer, Philip Sherrard, and Kallistos Ware (London: Faber and Faber, 1983), 185, cited by Laird, *Sunlit Absence*, 73.

8. Laird, *Sunlit Absence*, 17.

9. Dietrich Bonhoeffer, *Life Together* (New York: Harper & Row, 1954), 85.

Chapter 5: Room

1. Henri J. M. Nouwen, "Moving from Solitude to Community to Ministry," *Leadership Journal* (Spring 1995), 81, https://www.laidlaw.ac.nz/assets/Files-PDF-Word/Nouwen-Solitude-Community-Ministry.pdf.

2. Charles Stone, *Holy Noticing: The Bible, Your Brain, and the Mindful Space between Moments* (Chicago: Moody, 2019), 14.

3. Gerald Sittser, *Water from a Deep Well: Christian Spirituality from Early Martyrs to Modern Missionaries* (Downers Grove, IL: IVP Books, 2007), 83.

4. So the next time your kid gets in trouble and is told to go to their room, remind them on the way that even this penalty is a form of privilege.

5. Daniel J. Harrington, *Gospel of Matthew* (Collegeville, MN: Liturgical Press, 1991), 94.

6. Sittser, *Water from a Deep Well*, 83.

7. Bruce Demarest, *Seasons of the Soul: Stages of Spiritual Development* (Downers Grove, IL: InterVarsity, 2009), 114.

8. Martin S. Laird, *A Sunlit Absence: Silence, Awareness, and Contemplation* (New York: Oxford University Press, 2011), 40–41.

9. Charles Taylor, *A Secular Age* (Cambridge, MA: Belknap, 2007).

Chapter 6: Still

1. Zameena Mejia, "Steve Jobs: Here's What Most People Get Wrong about Focus," CNBC Make It, October 2, 2018, https://www.cnbc.com/2018/10/02/steve-jobs-heres-what-most-people-get-wrong-about-focus.html

2. Sister Ruth, quoted in George Appleton, ed., *The Oxford Book of Prayer* (Oxford: Oxford University Press, 1985), 8.

3. Richard Rohr, *Falling Upward: A Spirituality for the Two Halves of Life* (San Francisco: Jossey-Bass, 2011).

4. Augustine, *Exposition on Psalm 139*, chap. 15, in *Expositions on the Psalms*, trans. M. Boulding, The Works of Saint Augustine III/20 (Hyde Park, NY: New City, 2004), 297.

5. Cynthia Bourgeault, *Centering Prayer and Inner Awakening* (Cambridge, MA: Cowley, 2004), 32.

6. Bourgeault, *Centering Prayer*, 32.

7. Bourgeault, *Centering Prayer*, 32.

8. Dietrich Bonhoeffer, *God Is on the Cross: Reflections on Lent and Easter*, ed. Jana Riess (Louisville: Westminster John Knox, 2012), 8.

9. L. Paul Jensen, *Subversive Spirituality: Transforming Mission through the Collapse of Space and Time* (Eugene, OR: Pickwick, 2007), 86.

10. Martin S. Laird, *A Sunlit Absence: Silence, Awareness, and Contemplation* (New York: Oxford University Press, 2011), 42.

11. Laird, *Sunlit Absence*, 60.

12. Laird, *Sunlit Absence*, 60.

13. Henri J. M. Nouwen, "Moving from Solitude to Community to Ministry," *Leadership Journal* (Spring 1995), 81, https://www.laidlaw.ac.nz/assets/Files -PDF-Word/Nouwen-Solitude-Community-Ministry.pdf.

14. Laird, *Sunlit Absence*, 43.

15. Pete Greig, *How to Pray: A Simple Guide for Normal People* (Colorado Springs: NavPress, 2019), xiv.

Chapter 7: Groans

1. Marjorie J. Thompson, *Soul Feast: An Invitation to the Christian Spiritual Life* (Louisville: Westminster John Knox, 1995), locs. 545–47 of 2353. Kindle.

2. Douglas Moo, *The Epistle to the Romans*, New International Commentary on the New Testament (Grand Rapids: Eerdmans, 1996), 524.

3. Moo, *Epistle to the Romans*, 526.

4. Martin S. Laird, *A Sunlit Absence: Silence, Awareness, and Contemplation* (New York: Oxford University Press, 2011), 92.

Chapter 8: Dive

1. Martin S. Laird, *A Sunlit Absence: Silence, Awareness, and Contemplation* (New York: Oxford University Press, 2011), 90.

2. Cited by Tricia McCary Rhodes, *The Wired Soul: Finding Spiritual Balance in a Hyperconnected Age* (Colorado Springs: NavPress, 2016), loc. 962 of 2806. Kindle.

3. Teresa of Avila, *Interior Castle* 7.1, trans. Mirabai Starr (New York: Riverhead Books, 2003), 262.

4. Laird, *Sunlit Absence*, 22–23.

5. Daniel Goleman, *Focus: The Hidden Driver of Excellence* (New York: HarperCollins, 2013), 15.

6. Tadej (Elder Thaddeus) of Vitovnica, *Our Thoughts Determine Our Lives: The Life and Teachings of Elder Thaddeus of Vitovnica*, trans. Ana Smiljanic (Platina, CA: St. Herman of Alaska Brotherhood, 2009), loc. 723 of 2806. Kindle.

Chapter 9: Gaze

1. Marjorie J. Thompson, *Soul Feast: An Invitation to the Christian Spiritual Life* (Louisville: Westminster John Knox, 1995), locs. 723–24 of 2353. Kindle.

2. Kenneth E. Bailey, *Jesus through Middle Eastern Eyes: Cultural Studies in the Gospels* (Downers Grove, IL: IVP Academic, 2008), 112.

3. Carlo Carretto, *Letters from the Desert* (Maryknoll, NY: Orbis Books, 1972), locs. 637–39 of 1420. Kindle.

4. Francis de Sales, quoted in Aldous Huxley, *The Perennial Philosophy* (New York: Harper & Row, 1947), 285.

5. Martin S. Laird, *A Sunlit Absence: Silence, Awareness, and Contemplation* (New York: Oxford University Press, 2011), 92.

6. Laird, *Sunlit Absence*, 91.

7. Hans Urs von Balthasar, *Prayer*, trans. Graham Harrison (San Francisco: Ignatius, 1986), 24.

8. Henri J. M. Nouwen, "Moving from Solitude to Community to Ministry," *Leadership Journal* (Spring 1995), https://www.laidlaw.ac.nz/assets/Files-PDF-Word/Nouwen-Solitude-Community-Ministry.pdf.

9. Oliver Burkeman, "Attentional Commons," *New Philosopher* (August–October 2017), quoted in Michael S. Hyatt, *Free to Focus: A Total Productivity System to Achieve More by Doing Less* (Grand Rapids: Baker Books, 2019), 16.

Part 3: Neurology

1. For more info on Timothy Royer, see https://royerneuroscience.com.

2. Andrew Newberg and David Halpern, *The Rabbi's Brain: An Introduction to Jewish Neurotheology* (Nashville: Turner, 2018), 20.

3. Benedict Carey, *How We Learn: The Surprising Truth about When, Where, and Why It Happens* (New York: Random House, 2014), 3.

Chapter 10: Breath

1. Tricia McCary Rhodes, *The Wired Soul: Finding Spiritual Balance in a Hyperconnected Age* (Colorado Springs: NavPress, 2016), loc. 977 of 2397. Kindle.

2. Marc Dingman, *Your Brain, Explained: What Neuroscience Reveals about Your Brain and Its Quirks* (Boston: Nicholas Brealey, 2019), 31.

3. Charles Stone, *Holy Noticing: The Bible, Your Brain, and the Mindful Space between Moments* (Chicago: Moody, 2019), 72.

4. Augustine, *Expositions on the Book of Psalms*, in *A Library of Fathers of the Catholic Church* (London: Rivington, 1857), 167.

5. Dingman, *Your Brain, Explained*, 17.

Chapter 11: Stress

1. Charles Stone, *Holy Noticing: The Bible, Your Brain, and the Mindful Space between Moments* (Chicago: Moody, 2019).

2. Evelyn Underhill, *Evelyn Underhill: Essential Writings*, ed. Emilie Griffin (Maryknoll, NY: Orbis Books, 2003), 31.

3. Krystin Arneson, "How 'Feierabend' Helps Germans Disconnect from the Workday," BBC, *The Life Project* (blog), October 7, 2020, https://www.bbc.com/worklife/article/20200929-how-feierabend-helps-germans-disconnect-from-the-workday.

4. Arneson, "How 'Feierabend' Helps Germans."

5. Stone, *Holy Noticing*, 8.

6. Note that most neuroscientists today tend to resist oversimplifying the brain as distinct "centers." But it is true that certain areas of the brain specialize in specific functions.

7. Frank Lynn Meshberger, "An Interpretation of Michelangelo's Creation of Adam Based on Neuroanatomy," *Journal of the American Medical Association* 264, no. 14 (October 10, 1990): 1837–41.

8. Joshua Greene, *Moral Tribes: Emotion, Reason, and the Gap between Us and Them* (New York: Penguin, 2013), 126.

9. Bessel Van der Kolk, *The Body Keeps the Score: Brain, Mind, and Body in the Healing of Trauma* (New York: Penguin, 2014).

10. Bronwyn Fryer, "Are You Working Too Hard?," *Harvard Business Review*, November 2005, https://hbr.org/2005/11/are-you-working-too-hard.

11. Armita Golkar et al., "The Influence of Work-Related Chronic Stress on the Regulation of Emotion and on Functional Connectivity in the Brain," *PLOS ONE* 9, no. 9 (September 3, 2014), https://doi.org/10.1371/journal.pone.0104550.

12. Robert A. J. Signer and Sean J. Morrison, "Mechanisms That Regulate Stem Cell Aging and Life Span," *Cell Stem Cell* 12, no. 2 (February 7, 2013): 152–65, https://doi.org/10.1016/j.stem.2013.01.001.

13. National Institute for Health and Welfare, "Heavy Stress and Lifestyle Can Predict How Long We Live," Science Daily, March 11, 2020, https://www.sciencedaily.com/releases/2020/03/200311100857.htm.

14. Marc Dingman, *Your Brain, Explained: What Neuroscience Reveals about Your Brain and Its Quirks* (Boston: Nicholas Brealey, 2019), 98–99.

15. This quote is attributed to Luther but likely comes from an amalgamation of Luther and Charles Spurgeon. See Spurgeon's sermon "Degrees of Power attending the Gospel," Metropolitan Tabernacle, Newington, September 3, 1865, https://www.spurgeongems.org/sermon/chs648.pdf. See also James Swan, "Luther: I Have So Much to Do That I Shall Have to Spend the First Three Hours in Prayer," *Beggars All* (blog), June 10, 2019, https://beggarsallreformation.blogspot.com/2009/07/luther-i-have-so-much-to-do-that-i.html.

Chapter 12: Sleep

1. Nina Pullano, "How Many Hours of Sleep Is Enough? Age Chart Shows What You Need to Feel Rested," Inverse, February 1, 2020, https://www.inverse.com/mind-body/how-many-hours-of-sleep-do-you-need-to-feel-rested.

2. Marc Dingman, *Your Brain, Explained: What Neuroscience Reveals about Your Brain and Its Quirks* (Boston: Nicholas Brealey, 2019), 65.

3. Sourya C., "Roger Federer Sleeps 12 Hours a Day, Which Is Helping His Longevity," Sportskeeda, last modified May 18, 2020, https://www.sportskeeda.com/tennis/news-roger-federer-sleeps-12-hours-a-day-which-is-helping-his-longevity.

4. An insight I first learned from Doc.

5. Michael Hyatt, *Free to Focus: A Total Productivity System to Achieve More by Doing Less* (Grand Rapids: Baker Books, 2019), 37.

Conclusion

1. Andrew B. Newberg, *Neurotheology: How Science Can Enlighten Us about Spirituality* (New York: Columbia University Press, 2018), 129–30.

2. Newberg, *Neurotheology*, 129–30.

3. Newberg, *Neurotheology*, 131.

4. Sara W. Lazar et al., "Meditation Experience Is Associated with Increased Cortical Thickness," *Neuroreport* 16, no. 17 (November 28, 2005): 1893–97, www.ncbi.nlm.nih.gov/pmc/articles/PMC1361002.

5. Daniel Goleman and Richard J. Davidson, *Altered Traits: Science Reveals How Meditation Changes Your Mind, Brain, and Body* (New York: Avery, 2017), 250.

6. Goleman and Davidson, *Altered Traits*, 250.

7. Goleman and Davidson, *Altered Traits*, 251.

8. Goleman and Davidson, *Altered Traits*, 252.

9. Andrew B. Newberg and David Halpern, *The Rabbi's Brain: An Introduction to Jewish Neurotheology* (Nashville: Turner, 2018), 30.

Appendix A

1. In the first discussion, have participants ask the question "Why am I here?" Help them identify what they are seeking during this time away and invite them to pursue that aim.

2. If you have assigned readings, provide instructions after the practice and before dismissing for the next session.

3. See the Book of Common Prayer if you'd like to follow the Anglican tradition of prayers.

4. This is a twelve-hour period of silence that extends through breakfast. Spiritual reading and personal reflection are welcomed here.

BIBLIOGRAPHY

Appleton, George, ed. *The Oxford Book of Prayer*. Oxford: Oxford University Press, 1985.

Augustine. *St. Augustine on the Psalms*. Translated by Scholastica Hebgin and Felicitas Corrigan. Westminster, MD: Newman, 1960.

Bailey, Kenneth E. *Jesus through Middle Eastern Eyes: Cultural Studies in the Gospels*. Downers Grove, IL: IVP Academic, 2008.

Balthasar, Hans Urs von. *Prayer*. New York: Sheed & Ward, 1961.

Basil the Great. "Letter 2 (to Gregory of Nazianzus)." Translated by Roy J. Deferrari. Loeb Classical Library 190. Cambridge, MA: Harvard University Press, 1926.

Bloom, Anthony. *Beginning to Pray*. Cincinnati: St. Anthony Messenger, 2004.

Bonhoeffer, Dietrich. *God Is on the Cross: Reflections on Lent and Easter*. Edited by Jana Riess. Louisville: Westminster John Knox, 2012.

———. *Life Together*. New York: Harper & Row, 1954.

Bourgeault, Cynthia. *Centering Prayer and Inner Awakening.* Cambridge, MA: Cowley, 2004.

Carretto, Carlo. *Letters from the Desert.* Maryknoll, NY: Orbis Books, 1972. Kindle.

Chepesiuk, Ron. "Decibel Hell: The Effects of Living in a Noisy World." *Environmental Health Perspectives* 113, no. 1 (January 2005): A34–A41, https://www.ncbi.nlm.nih.gov/pmc/articles/PMC1253729.

Demarest, Bruce. *Seasons of the Soul: Stages of Spiritual Development.* Downers Grove, IL: InterVarsity, 2009.

Dreher, Rod. *The Benedict Option: A Strategy for Christians in a Post-Christian Nation.* New York: Penguin, 2018.

Eldredge, John. *Get Your Life Back: Everyday Practices for a World Gone Mad.* Nashville: Thomas Nelson, 2020. Kindle.

Goleman, Daniel. *Focus: The Hidden Driver of Excellence.* New York: HarperCollins, 2013.

Goleman, Daniel, and Richard J. Davidson. *Altered Traits: Science Reveals How Meditation Changes Your Mind, Brain, and Body.* New York: Avery, 2017.

Greig, Pete. *How to Pray: A Simple Guide for Normal People.* Colorado Springs: NavPress, 2019.

Harrington, Daniel J. *The Gospel of Matthew.* Collegeville, MN: Liturgical Press, 1991.

Holder, Arthur G. *Christian Spirituality: The Classics.* London: Routledge, 2009.

Hyatt, Michael S. *Free to Focus: A Total Productivity System to Achieve More by Doing Less.* Grand Rapids: Baker Books, 2019.

Jensen, L. Paul. *Subversive Spirituality: Transforming Mission through the Collapse of Space and Time.* Eugene, OR: Pickwick, 2007.

Laird, Martin S. *A Sunlit Absence: Silence, Awareness, and Contemplation.* New York: Oxford University Press, 2011.

Mulholland, M. Robert, Jr. *The Deeper Journey: The Spirituality of Discovering Your True Self.* Downers Grove, IL: IVP Books, 2006.

Muller, Wayne. *Sabbath: Finding Rest, Renewal, and Delight in Our Busy Lives.* New York: Bantam, 2000.

Newberg, Andrew B. *Neurotheology: How Science Can Enlighten Us about Spirituality.* New York: Columbia University Press, 2018.

Newberg, Andrew B., and David Halpern. *The Rabbi's Brain: An Introduction to Jewish Neurotheology.* Nashville: Turner, 2018.

Newberg, Andrew B., and Mark Robert Waldman. *How God Changes Your Brain: Breakthrough Findings from a Leading Neuroscientist.* New York: Ballantine, 2010.

Norris, Kathleen. *Acedia and Me: A Marriage, Monks, and a Writer's Life.* New York: Penguin, 2008.

Nouwen, Henri J. M. *The Genesee Diary: Report from a Trappist Monastery.* Garden City, NY: Doubleday, 1976.

———. "Moving from Solitude to Community to Ministry," *Leadership Journal* (Spring 1995), 81–87, https://www.laidlaw.ac.nz/assets/Files-PDF-Word/Nouwen-Solitude-Community-Ministry.pdf.

———. *The Return of the Prodigal Son: A Story of Homecoming.* London: Darton, Longman & Todd, 2008.

Oden, Thomas C. *The Rebirth of Orthodoxy.* San Francisco: HarperSanFrancisco, 2003.

Peterson, Eugene H. *The Contemplative Pastor: Returning to the Art of Spiritual Direction.* Grand Rapids: Eerdmans, 1996. Kindle.

Rhodes, Tricia McCary. *The Wired Soul: Finding Spiritual Balance in a Hyperconnected Age.* Colorado Springs: NavPress, 2016. Kindle.

Sacks, Jonathan, ed. and trans. *The Koren Siddur*. New Milford, CT: Koren, 2009.

Sharot, Tali. *The Influential Mind: What the Brain Reveals about Our Power to Change Others*. New York: Henry Holt, 2018.

Simon, Herbert A. "Designing Organizations for an Information-Rich World." In *Economics of Communication and Information*, edited by Donald M. Lamberton, 187–202. Brookfield, VT: Edward Elgar, 1996.

Sittser, Gerald Lawson. *Water from a Deep Well: Christian Spirituality from Early Martyrs to Modern Missionaries*. Downers Grove, IL: IVP Books, 2007.

Smith, Gordon T. *Called to Be Saints: An Invitation to Christian Maturity*. Downers Grove, IL: IVP Academic, 2014.

Stone, Charles. *Holy Noticing: The Bible, Your Brain, and the Mindful Space between Moments*. Chicago: Moody, 2019.

Tadej (Elder Thaddeus) of Vitovnica. *Our Thoughts Determine Our Lives: The Life and Teachings of Elder Thaddeus of Vitovnica*. Translated by Ana Smiljanic. Platina, CA: St. Herman of Alaska Brotherhood, 2009. Kindle.

Teresa of Avila. *The Interior Castle*. Translated by Mirabai Starr. New York: Riverhead Books, 2003.

Thibodeaux, Mark E. *Armchair Mystic: Easing into Contemplative Prayer*. Cincinnati: St. Anthony Messenger Press, 2001.

Thompson, Marjorie J. *Soul Feast: An Invitation to the Christian Spiritual Life*. Louisville: Westminster John Knox, 1995. Kindle.

Wallace, David Foster. *The Pale King: An Unfinished Novel*. New York: Back Bay Books, 2012.

Zahl, David. *Seculosity: How Career, Parenting, Technology, Food, Politics, and Romance Became Our New Religion and What to Do about It*. Minneapolis: Fortress, 2019.

Made in the USA
Columbia, SC
15 July 2023